The
NEW ORLEANS
CHEF'S TABLE

The
NEW ORLEANS
CHEF'S TABLE

EXTRAORDINARY RECIPES FROM THE CRESCENT CITY

LORIN GAUDIN
WITH PHOTOGRAPHY BY ROMNEY CARUSO

Globe
Pequot

Guilford, Connecticut

This book is dedicated to the City of New Orleans . . .
A place that took me in, embraced me hard, and slipped deep into
my soul to become an indelible part of my DNA and my home.
I love New Orleans—the people, the music, the culture, and of
course, the food—and I am grateful she loves me right back.

Globe
Pequot

An imprint of The Rowman & Littlefield Publishing Group, Inc.
4501 Forbes Blvd., Ste. 200
Lanham, MD 20706
www.rowman.com

Distributed by NATIONAL BOOK NETWORK

British Library Cataloguing in Publication Information Available

Library of Congress Cataloging-in-Publication Data Available

ISBN 978-1-4930-4440-5 (hardback)
ISBN 978-1-4930-4441-2 (e-book)

♾™ The paper used in this publication meets the minimum requirements
of American National Standard for Information Sciences—Permanence of
Paper for Printed Library Materials, ANSI/NISO Z39.48-1992.

Restaurants and chefs often come and go, and menus are ever-changing.
We recommend you call ahead to obtain current information before
visiting any of the establishments in this book.

CONTENTS

ACKNOWLEDGMENTS

I want to thank first and foremost my husband Andre and sons Collins and Remy, who all tolerate my food craziness, the constant chatter, piles of cookbooks, obsession with food and cooking, and who have supported me unfailingly in all my culinary endeavors. I must thank my sisters and brother for being as food-crazy as me and always letting me in on the latest and greatest places to eat where they live—it gives me a great national perspective. My mom and dad get thanks for the genetics that made me who I am and am not. I also want to thank my dear departed mother-in-law, Janice, who was so special to me and taught me many family recipes that stretch back more than a hundred years. She would be proud to know that those dishes remain an important

part of Gaudin meal rituals. To all the photographers whose talent, energy, excitement, and hunger made this project pop with color and taste: I am in awe. It is said we first eat with our eyes, and the drool-inducing food photographs prove that perfectly. Finally, I am forever grateful to the gob-smackingly brilliant and fun chefs of New Orleans, who bring tears to my eyes with their stunning art and whom I adore.

Additional Photo Credits

Photography of the following list of places are courtesy of the restaurants: Arnaud's, Carrollton Market, Cavan, Clancy's, The Country Club, Del Fuego, Delgado Community College Culinary School, Galatoire's, Haydel's Bake Shop, Heard Dat Kitchen, Hobnobber Café, Jack Rose (Randy Schimdt), Mais Arepas, Mayhew Bakery, McClure's Barbecue, Piece of Meat, and Tujague's. Special credit goes to contributors Isaac Arjonella, Sara Essex Bradley, Denny Culbert, Gabrielle Milone, Randy Schmidt, and Eugenie Uh.

Photography on pages 51, 140-141, 144, 146 © Getty Images

Photo of Lorin Gaudin on page 147 by Remi Gaudin

INTRODUCTION

"In New Orleans, we can be eating a meal while talking about another meal or cooking or restaurants, and simultaneously planning the next meal. Food obsessed, that's what we are."

—*Everyone in New Orleans*

It is well established that New Orleanians are food obsessed. Some say that food is our lingua franca, the way we communicate, our working language, the way we connect to one another. And that is the absolute truth. It is the norm to hear tables of diners talking food, cooking, favored restaurants, new restaurants, the demise of beloved restaurants, the next restaurant, markets, local products, and food finds—all with a mouth full of food from the plate immediately on the table. The spirit of New Orleans is reflected in her cooking and restaurants, her people, and her multiplicity of cultures.

The city has long been known for certain foods and dishes—beignets, jambalaya, gumbo, boudin, crawfish—our regional cuisine, what the national food press has called New Orleans's "one menu." It is true that we do have that menu, and we do it proudly and beautifully, but New Orleans is a very exciting food city. We have more, do more, explore more, and have created a bunch of "menus" deserving of attention. No one has abandoned tradition in the name of progress—the two walk hand in hand. We embrace our food traditions, eat lovingly and happily from a plate of red beans and rice or let the juices run down our arms from a messy roast beef po-boy, but that doesn't stop us from diving into compressed melon and icy-cool avocado "dippin' dots"; we're immersed in it, deeply. I don't believe that any of our foods is threatened with extinction—we're too stubborn and love ourselves too much to let that happen. Food here is revered religiously and consumed passionately. The number of sit-down

restaurants in the New Orleans area is staggering and shows no signs of slowing in growth; and still, our population hasn't returned to what it was in 2005! Fewer people and an enormous number of restaurants! That's a phenomenon in and of itself.

Yes, we love our food. We love the Gulf that gives us an incredible variety of finfish, crab, shrimp, and oysters, our waterways and rice fields from which spring crawfish, our alluvial soil that gives glorious Creole tomatoes with their stunning sunshine-bright flavor. We adore our elders and families who cook and remind us of important recipes: the flame keepers who gather in organizations, open museums, and offer exhibits and collections for us to experience, so we never forget a sip or a bite. And New Orleans is experiencing a culinary evolution too. As the template of our city shifts, grows and renovates, restores and reinvigorates, so do the food, cooking, and restaurants.

New Orleans is a fascinating place. Natives and long-standing transplants stand shoulder-to-shoulder with the new locals, and there is no denying a decidedly younger demographic who contribute a fresh look and palate. Many adventurous cooks, chefs and those clamoring to be restaurant owners, have successfully taken the leap into the industry, in parts of New Orleans that were previously quiet or undeveloped. This book covers some of everything—well-loved "grande dame" restaurants, places that have been around and refreshed, places that have made a local mark on our restaurant landscape but aren't as well known, and those that are brand new.

New Orleans is nestled in the Parish of Orleans, positioned on the crescent of the Mississippi River and mapped by neighborhoods. Each of these neighborhoods has a distinct tone, and all are filled cheek-by-jowl with historic homes—mansions and shotguns, pristine or time- and weather-worn, many family-owned for hundreds of years—mixed with commerce. It is a New Orleans hallmark that neighborhoods are both residential and commercial. The architectural styles reflect Spanish and French rule as well as accommodations to our tropical climate that swelters in summer and withstands the vagaries of catastrophic storms.

Organization

This book covers a lot of New Orleans culinary and geographic ground. New Orleans is a city of neighborhoods and people from myriad cultures and all walks of life, inextricably and lovingly linked together. A lot has happened since the initial publication of this book and interestingly a lot has stayed the same. So many restaurants have come and gone, the numbers are staggering.

Nonetheless, the included restaurants and recipes cut a wide swath across the Metro New Orleans area, and there's even one located in Metairie—a New Orleans suburb where my husband was raised—because it is an important part of the culinary and cultural landscape for Italian family, food and spiritual connection. All-in-all the book is a delicious tour of our dining and local culture. New Orleans is a sensorial place with very specific identifying aromas that signify. The spicy scent of cayenne, herbs, and lemon means crawfish, crab, or shrimp season, while the air thick with fried chicken's pungent, mouthwateringly greasy scent is all about Mardi Gras (or "Carnival" if you're a native). There's the dusty sagelike aroma of swamp bay that hangs on the dark of sultry summer evenings, and of course the musty, wet-wood funk of neighborhood bars that beg for an icy beer or soothing highball. By engaging all five senses, it is possible to see, hear, feel, smell, and taste the distinguishing differences throughout New Orleans. New Orleans is intensely tactile; even walking Jackson Square can evoke the sound of nineteenth-century heels clicking on the slate, or cause the weighty layers of historic events both glorious and heart-wrenching to be felt on the skin. Food, dining, and cuisine are a natural extension of the experience—yes, New Orleans is an experience—filled with people often referred to as "characters." New Orleans is a living story. And this is my version.

This book is about my on-going love and respect for our chefs and restaurants of New Orleans, about the beauty that is Louisiana product, smarts, creativity, and deliciousness. It's about the new and old way we eat in New Orleans, dispelling that one-menu moniker, screaming from the rooftops that while we love our culinary traditions, there is more going on here. Come visit, wander the neighborhoods, and dine extensively and comprehensively—it's so worth it. Try the dishes for which we are famous, or today's interpretations; the ethnic foods; the food trucks; the produce and prepared foods from our extensive farmers' markets; poboys and yakamein from corner stores; classic cocktails; or plate lunches from a mom-and-pop cafe. There is no wrong. This is a delicious city, my home. Come fall head-over-heels in love, a deep foodie love, with New Orleans. And if you can't visit, then cook up a recipe or two and savor the flavor. You'll fall in love just the same.

COMMANDER'S PALACE

1403 Washington Avenue
(504) 899-8221
commanderspalace.com

The Garden District of New Orleans is a lovely place, filled with grand mansions, modest homes, old families, and one of our city's grandest "grande dame" restaurants. The post–Hurricane Katrina renovation of Commander's continues to lend elegance, but there is also a more approachable feeling to the place. Executive Chef Tory McPhail enhances that vibration. The restaurant continues to serve its amazing turtle soup and bread pudding soufflé—the world would be lost without them—but there are also Tory's bolder explorations and cooking fancies that appear on the menu to bring a freshness reflecting progress without abandoning tradition. Chef Tory and the Commander's Palace owners, the late Miss Ella, her daughter Ti Martin, her cousin Lally Brennan, exude charm, grace, and fun. The cocktails have a kick, thanks to the Cocktail Chicks (Ti and Lally) and the stellar bar team. Everything is sourced locally, regionally, and/or from the United States; that's long been the way things are done, and now Commander's Palace does things with a current feel. 25-cent-martini lunch, anyone?

CRAWFISH BOIL VICHYSSOISE
(YIELDS 1 GALLON/20 PORTIONS; MAY BE HALVED)

For the soup:

8 ounces boiled crawfish, pureed

2½ pounds red bliss or any thin-skinned, small new potatoes

4 ounces leeks, green tops removed, washed well and sliced

4 ounces carrots, peeled and chopped

4 ounces celery, stalks only, washed and chopped

1 ounce Zatarain's crawfish boil powder

3 quarts whole milk

1 ounce sugarcane vinegar

For the garnish:

1 pound button mushrooms, in small dice

1 pound corn kernels

4 ounces garlic cloves, peeled

4 ounces sweet potatoes, in small dice

3 pounds crawfish tails, lightly grilled

20 whole boiled crawfish

2 ounces red chili oil

To make the soup: Combine all ingredients in a pot and bring to a simmer. Cook for 40 minutes or until potatoes are cooked through and very tender. Working in small batches, puree the soup in a high-powered blender until very smooth and creamy. Pass through a chinois and adjust thickness and seasoning as necessary. This soup is intended to be served at room temperature.

To garnish the soup: Prepare a bubbling pot of crawfish boil, and an ice bath of crawfish boil water. Blanch the mushrooms, corn, garlic, and sweet potatoes separately in the crawfish boil until al dente, and then shock them in the ice bath to stop the cooking. Combine with the crawfish tails and spoon into soup bowls. Pour 6 ounces of soup around the garnish and place a whole boiled crawfish on top. Finish by adding tiny drops of chili oil to the surface of the soup for added kick.

GULF SHRIMP & BLUE CRAB ENCHILADAS

(SERVES 8 AS APPETIZER, 4 AS ENTREE)

For the enchilada sauce:

8 tomatoes, chopped

1 onion, diced

1 chipotle chili, soaked for 10 minutes in warm
  water

1 teaspoon cayenne pepper

½ bunch cilantro

½ cup vinegar

1 teaspoon ground cumin

2 cloves garlic

Salt to taste

For the enchiladas:

4 teaspoons butter

2 cloves garlic, minced

1 large onion, diced

2 jalapeños, seeds removed, diced

2 large tomatoes, diced

Kernels from 1 ear of corn

1 cup cooked black beans

½ bunch cilantro

16 shrimp (36/40 count), peeled, deveined, and
  chopped

½ pound blue crab meat, picked free of shell

½ teaspoon ground cumin

½ teaspoon ground coriander

Salt and pepper to taste

2 cups corn oil

8 corn tortillas

2 cups enchilada sauce

8 ounces Idiazabal cheese, grated

To make the sauce: Place all ingredients in heavy saucepan with 2 cups water and cook for 20 minutes on medium heat. Remove from heat and puree in blender until smooth. Season with salt to your liking.

To make the enchiladas: Place a large sauté pan on medium heat. Add butter to pan. Add garlic, onion, jalapeños, and tomatoes. Sauté until onions are translucent. Add corn, beans, and cilantro. Cook for 4–5 minutes. Add shrimp and crab and cook for 2–3 minutes. Add cumin and coriander and then season with salt and pepper. Allow to cool.

Preheat oven to 375°F. Heat the corn oil to 275°F in large pot. Dip each tortilla in the warm oil for 15 seconds or until it is pliable, then coat it in enchilada sauce. Place 3 ounces of shrimp and crab filling on the tortilla and roll into a cylinder. Place in a heatproof dish.

When all tortillas are filled, sprinkle with cheese and more sauce. Bake for 5–7 minutes or until cheese melts.

"COMPRESSED" STRAWBERRIES

(SERVES 4)

For the strawberries:

24 Ponchatoula strawberries, hulled

1 cup strawberry jam

For the Jell-O pearls:

2 cups vegetable oil

1 package strawberry Jell-O

For the whipped cream:

1 cup heavy cream

½ cup strawberry jam

For the strawberry Hurricane cocktail:

1 ounce light rum

1 ounce dark rum

1 ounce pineapple juice

1 ounce orange juice

2 ounces strawberry jam

For assembly:

Compressed strawberries, halved

Strawberry whipped cream

4 ounces strawberry Jell-O pearls

1 package strawberry Pop Rocks

4 strawberry Pixy Stix

4 ounces strawberry Hurricane cocktail

4 fresh mint sprigs

Powdered sugar in a shaker

To compress the strawberries: Place the berries in a medium bowl, rinse briefly under cool tap water, and drain very well. Add 1 cup of the strawberry jam and toss to coat evenly. Place the berries in a heavy Cryovac bag and vacuum-seal it. Break the seal on the corner of the bag and reseal 2 more times to drive the jam into the inside of the berry. Finally, after the third compression, leave the bag sealed for 4 hours to marinate.

To make the pearls: Place vegetable oil in the freezer in a shallow baking dish and chill for 1–2 hours. Prepare strawberry-flavored Jell-O according to package instructions, temper it in an ice bath, and stir constantly with a rubber spatula until it just starts to get thick. The Jell-O should be about 50–60°F. Pour the thickened jelly into a squeeze bottle with a narrow tip. Remove the chilled oil from the freezer and place on a countertop. Working back and forth and about 1 foot above the surface of the oil, inject the Jell-O into the oil to form tiny pearls. Pour the Jell-O and oil through a fine strainer to separate. Drain for 5 minutes in the refrigerator so the pearls are very dry and free of oil.

To make the whipped cream: Pour cream and ½ cup of strawberry jam into a bowl and whisk quickly to thicken. Note that different brands of jam have different sugar content, so adjust amount as necessary.

To make the strawberry Hurricane: Place all ingredients into an ice-filled cocktail shaker. Shake well to blend the cocktail and dissolve the jam. Strain.

To assemble: Break the seal of the compressed strawberries, pour them into a bowl, and slice each berry in half. Smear the strawberry whipped cream in the center of four dessert plates. Arrange the sliced berries, cut side up, along the whipped cream, then garnish the tops with the pearls, Pop Rocks, and Pixy Stix. Place a small hurricane glass on each plate and pour in the cocktail. Finish with mint sprigs and a light dusting of powdered sugar.

CARROLLTON MARKET

8132 Hampson Street
(504) 265-0421
carrolltonmarket.com

In the Riverbend near Loyola (my alma mater) and Tulane Universities, Chef Jason Goodenough opened Carrollton Market. Chef Jason, a larger-than-life (he's a sturdy 6'5"!!), award-winning Chef (New Orleans Magazine Chef of the Year, 2018, for one), is highly sought out for regional and national festival cooking demonstrations, television appearances and events. He's equal parts smart, fun, kind, and loud; he's also immensely talented. When Chef Jason takes on a cause, it's full throttle. He is a major supporter of at-risk youth/adult organizations such as Cafe Hope and Okra Abbey, working to give meals, advice and service. His restaurant, Carrollton Market pays homage to approachable, yet sophisticated French cuisine with a local twist. His restaurant is full of hum and buzz, and busy. There is a small but serious bar with a very good wine list and cleverly crafted cocktails. Chef Jason digs deep to locally-source products for his dishes. Carrollton Market's Chef de Cuisine, Justin Ferguson is a true gem—his Southern roots, smarts and mad skills play a big role in the restaurant's success. There is a solid team at Carrollton Market, pushing out bold brunches with giant cinnamon rolls that have been featured by Food & Wine magazine, buttery Parker House—style rolls, special menu family style dinners, and loads of fun with the Chef's last name gracing dishes that are more than "Goodenough."

OYSTERS GOODENOUGH
FLASH—FRIED GULF OYSTERS, BENTON'S BACON,
CREAMED LEEKS, BÉARNAISE

(YIELDS 10 OYSTERS)

For the oyster:

10 large, pre-shucked Gulf oysters (cleaned and sanitized oyster shells or ceramic oyster shells)

2 cups of panko breadcrumbs, ground in a blender until it has the feel of flour (we call this panko flour)

Salt to taste

For the creamed leeks:

5 large leeks, green parts removed, whites quartered lengthwise

1½ cup heavy cream

½ cup dry white wine

½ stick butter, unsalted

½ pound Allen Benton's Bacon (or your favorite smoky bacon)

For the Béarnaise sauce:

4 egg yolks

1 pound butter, unsalted, melted, skimmed and decanted

½ cup white wine

1 ounce tarragon vinegar

1½ large tarragon stems

1 large shallot, thinly sliced

½ tablespoon peppercorn mignonette

Lemon juice to taste

¼ cup (at least) chopped tarragon

To cook the oysters: dredge oysters in the panko flour, fry in 375°F oil until golden brown (30–45 seconds). Remove from oil and season with salt.

To prepare the creamed leeks: Thinly slice leeks and soak in water, agitating regularly to remove dirt and debris. Drain thoroughly in a colander or salad spinner. Sweat leeks over low heat until very soft but not caramelized at all, 20-ish minutes. Turn up heat to medium. Add white wine. Reduce by ⅔. Add 1 cup heavy cream. Reduce by half. Add last half-cup of heavy cream. Reduce by half or until mixture is very thick but not broken.

Separately, thinly julienne bacon and render over low to medium heat until crispy. Drain fat and reserve.

Combine white wine, tarragon vinegar, stems, shallot and mignonette in a small saucepan. Reduce liquid until dry. Remove pan from heat and add ⅓ cup water to rehydrate. Strain through a chinois fine.

To prepare the Béarnaise: Place half of reduction, yolks, and ¼ cup room temp water in a large bowl. Beat over a double boiler until fluffy and ribbon stage. Ensure mixture is hot enough to set as well. Remove from heat and emulsify in decanted butter fat. Adjust consistency with warm water; too thick and sauce will break.

Finish with salt, chopped tarragon and adjust acidity with lemon juice or remaining reduction. Hold warm but not hot.

To serve: Place a heaping tablespoon leak mixture on clean oyster shell. Top with bacon, a fried oyster, and a hearty tablespoon of Béarnaise. Garnish with tarragon and serve immediately.

EMERIL'S DELMONICO

1300 Saint Charles Avenue
(504) 525-4937
emerilsrestaurants.com/emerils-delmonico

When Chef Emeril bought the old-time restaurant space called Delmonico, those New Orleanians who were of an age were shaken. As is the way here, the thought of change didn't sit well. Ah, but we're talking about Emeril Lagasse, and what resulted was a stunningly renovated and restored building that caters to fine dining, in the way the original Delmonico envisioned, only a tad more contemporary Creole with some global inspiration. Meats are aged on the premises, and the menu features big cuts of beef, as well as lamb, duck, and fish plucked from the Gulf. The cocktail lounge is fun, with live music on the weekends and great Sazeracs to sip.

EMERIL'S DELMONICO PORK CHEEKS WITH CREOLE DIRTY RICE
Recipe Courtesy Emeril Lagasse
Emeril's Food of Love Productions, 2008
(SERVES 4)

2½ pounds pork cheeks, cleaned and trimmed
of all tough membranes

8 cloves garlic

6 sprigs fresh thyme

1½ tablespoons kosher salt

1 tablespoon coarsely ground black pepper

1 tablespoon coriander seeds

Vegetable oil as needed

1 cup flour, or more as needed for dusting

2 tablespoons unsalted butter

1 recipe Creole Dirty Rice, for serving
(recipe follows)

Preheat the oven to 325°F.

Place the pork cheeks, garlic, thyme, salt, pepper, and coriander seeds in a baking dish just large enough to hold the pork in one layer. Add enough vegetable oil to completely cover the pork. Cover the dish tightly with aluminum foil and bake until cheeks are fork-tender, usually 4–4½ hours. (This

will depend on the size of the pork cheeks you are able to procure, so check periodically during the cooking time.) When the pork is tender, remove from the oven and allow to cool in the oil. Once cool, remove the cheeks from the oil and pat dry with paper towels. (Oil may be strained and used for another purpose.)

Dust the cheeks lightly with flour. Heat a medium sauté pan over medium-high heat. When hot, add 2 tablespoons of oil to the pan, and when oil is hot, add 1 tablespoon of the butter. Sauté the cheeks, in batches if necessary, until golden brown on all sides, 2–3 minutes. Remove from the pan and repeat with remaining cheeks, adding more vegetable oil and remaining butter if necessary.

Serve the cheeks hot, with the Creole Dirty Rice.

CREOLE DIRTY RICE

Recipe Courtesy Emeril Lagasse
Emeril's Food of Love Productions, 2008

(SERVES 4)

1 tablespoon vegetable oil

1 tablespoon butter

½ cup chopped yellow onion

½ cup chopped bell pepper

¼ pound ground pork

¼ pound chicken livers, pureed

2 bay leaves

1 tablespoon finely chopped jalapeño

½ teaspoon salt

¼ teaspoon ground coriander

¼ teaspoon ground cumin

¼ teaspoon cayenne

2 cups cooked long grain white rice

¼ cup beef stock or canned low-sodium beef broth

Dash of Tabasco, or other Louisiana hot sauce, or to taste

In a large skillet, heat the oil over medium-high heat. When hot, add the butter, onions, and bell peppers and sauté vegetables until tender and lightly caramelized, 4–6 minutes. Add the pork and cook, using the spoon to break the pork into small pieces, until well browned, 1–2 minutes. Add the liver puree, bay leaves, jalapeño, salt, coriander, cumin, and cayenne and cook until liver is cooked through and spices are fragrant, 2–3 minutes. Add the rice and beef stock and continue to cook, stirring, until well combined and heated through, 2–3 minutes longer. Adjust the seasoning if necessary and add hot sauce to taste.

THE COUNTRY CLUB

634 Louisa Street, (504) 945-0742
Thecountryclubneworleans.com

This grand, Bywater Italianate mansion was lovingly restored and renovated. Filled with art, color and beautifully designed, The Country Club (AKA "The Club") is well known for its big dining space, interior bar, an outdoor space with a pool, bar and outdoor kitchen. This is an incredible place. Fun, frivolous, beautiful and delicious. The Executive Chef, Chris Barbato, has an extensive history in New Orleans, having worked for many years at Commander's Palace, before creating the menus at "The Club." He's truly amazing—thoughtful to season, clever in developing dishes, keen on local sourcing when possible and he never stops moving. His wife Lisa Barbato is the pastry chef and she too has an impressive culinary pedigree. Together, Chefs Chris and Lisa are a true culinary tour de force. Along with their kitchen team, actually the entire Club staff, this crew is

about as talented, friendly and efficient as they come. Reserve a table for Saturday's "Drag Brunch" and dig in to gorgeous egg dishes and bottomless mimosas. For dinner service, Chef Chris' menu has sophisticated dishes like saffron-scented steamed mussels or duck fat roasted chicken. Save room for dessert. Lisa's ice creams, fruit cobblers and silky panna cottas are divine. There's a fantastic poolside menu too, creative cocktails, Happy Hours . . . it's endless. Sense a theme? The food, drink and ambiance are incredible, but the overarching theme is fun.

CRAB BEIGNETS WITH SAFFRON AIOLI
(YIELDS 30 1OZ BEIGNETS)

2 tablespoons shallots, minced

¼ cup cream cheese, room temp.

¼ cup mascarpone, room temp.

¼ cup pepper jack, shredded

¼ cup parmesan, grated

1 green onion, sliced thin

1 teaspoon kosher salt

1 teaspoon black pepper

1 packet sazon con azafran

8oz crab meat, clean of shells

4 teaspoons sofrito (recipe below)

4 cups vegetable oil for frying

Place all the ingredients in a medium bowl and gently mix until it is all evenly incorporated, you want to keep the crab lumps as intact as you can. Next, using a 1oz ice cream scoop, scoop balls and place on a parchment lined sheet pan. Place in the refrigerator until needed. You can make these a day in advance. You may also freeze the crab balls on a parchment lined sheet tray. Once the balls are frozen, place them in a zip lock freezer bag.

For the sofrito:

1 red bell pepper, seeded and chopped

1 medium onion, chopped

4 garlic cloves

½ bunch cilantro

Pinch of salt and pepper

Place all the ingredients and puree. You only need a small amount for this recipe, but this is a great condiment to have on hand. You can freeze this in ice cube trays and add it to soups, sauces, meats.

For the beer batter:

1 cup all-purpose flour

⅓ cup corn starch

1 tablespoon baking powder

½ teaspoon salt

1 cup beer (lager)

Mix all the dry ingredients in a medium bowl. Add the beer a little at a time, until the batter is just thicker than a pancake batter. Let it sit for 30 minutes.

For the saffron aioli:

2 tablespoons hot water

½ teaspoon saffron, crushed

1 garlic clove, minced

½ cup mayonnaise

1 teaspoon fresh lemon juice

salt and pepper to taste

Pour the hot water over the crushed saffron. (It is important to crush the saffron so that it will release more of its essence and give your aioli a beautiful, golden color.) Let this sit for 10 minutes. Add the remaining ingredients. Taste for seasoning.

continued . . .

To fry the crab beignets and serve:

Heat 4 cups of vegetable oil in a heavy-bottomed pot or deep sided cast iron skillet to 350°F. Drop the crab balls into the beer batter, making sure they are completely coated. In batches, fry the beignets in the hot oil until they are golden brown (1–2 minutes). Remove with slotted spoon. Serve with the Saffron Aioli.

MADAME MARIE LAVEAU FLOAT

For the shot:

2½ ounces coffee liqueur

2 ounces port

2 ounces brandy

1 ounce Fernet-Branca liqueur

For the brownies:

½ pound butter

1 teaspoon vanilla extract

8 ounces bittersweet chocolate

¾ cup all-purpose flour

1½ cups granulated sugar

pinch of salt

4 eggs (lightly whisked)

For the chocolate sauce:

½ cup water

½ cup sugar

¼ cup light corn syrup

⅓ cup cocoa powder

1 ounce semisweet chocolate

Vanilla Ice cream and whipped cream (your favorites)

To make the shot: Mix all the ingredients together. Set aside.

To make the brownies: Place the butter, vanilla, and chocolate in a saucepot and heat on low until melted and incorporated. Remove from heat and add the sugar, mix with a wooden spoon until combined. Mix in the salt and eggs. Add the flour and stir until combined. Pour into a parchment lined 8 x 8-inch pan. Bake at 350°F for 40 minutes. When cool, cut into 1 x 1-inch squares.

To prepare the chocolate sauce: Place all the ingredients into a medium bottom saucepan. Heat over low heat until all melted and incorporated.

To serve: Place a scoop of vanilla in an ice cream dish. Pour an ounce (or two) of the Marie Laveau shot over the ice cream. Top with whipped cream, brownies and chocolate sauce.

MAIS AREPAS

1200 Carondolet Street
(504) 523-6247

In Central City, just off the Saint Charles Avenue streetcar line sits this gem-of-a-restaurant. The food is rooted in rustic, homey Colombian cuisine, yet it is elevated by the creativity and passion of Chef David Mantilla. With his partner Matt Blevins, these guys have created a restaurant oasis, a step into Colombia without leaving Louisiana. Chef David grows a lot of his own vegetables for specials and he's always on the hunt for sourcing foods from his homeland. The interior of the restaurant is lively, with art-filled walls; there's Latin dance music playing, the vibe is up and the cocktails are cold. As for the food . . . the street corn (*Mais De La Rueda*) is among their most popular dishes and it is truly addictive. If I could ever talk David or Matt into giving me their sauce recipe . . . it'll never happen. Ah well, there is so much to love here: perfectly tender boiled shrimp topped with pickled red onions and a fresh salsa-cocktail sauce combo atop avocado; marinated and grilled meats, chicken and seafood, plantains and cheese-filled split arepas for hefty sandwiches; brothy, soul-soothing ajiaco soup (chicken, corn, potato, tubers, etc); fried yucca and spicy chorizo sausage . . . I could go on. The desserts are also spectacular—flan with passion fruit syrup and fresh fruit or a soft and sweet tres leches cake—and all are gluten free. In fact, most everything here is gluten free. The Colombian red beans and rice recipe is very similar to the familiar New Orleanians favorite, and perfect to make on Mondays when Mais Arepas is closed.

COLOMBIAN–STYLE CRANBERRY BEANS

(SERVES 6-8)

2½ cups cranberry beans

½ red onion, diced

½ green bell pepper, diced

½ red bell pepper, diced

1 tablespoon garlic, minced

1 green plantain, diced

½ cup pork belly, diced

2 tablespoon kosher salt

1 tablespoon ground black pepper

1 tablespoon ground cumin

1 tablespoon ground achiote

2 quarts unsalted beef stock

Put all the ingredients in a pressure cooker and cook over medium-high heat for about 30 minutes. After 30 minutes, add water if necessary and keep cooking over medium-low heat for 15 more minutes or until beans have softened.

GALATOIRE'S

Bourbon Street
(504) 520-8311
Galatoires.com

One of the French Quarter's restaurant "grandes dames," Galatoire's has been in business since 1905. It is a place that has to be experienced as well as tasted for dishes that are shining examples of culinary history and yet manage to be relevant today. True French Creole cuisine, extraordinary service, and on the main dining floor a room with hum, buzz, and history. The spirit of Galatoire's remains blessedly unchanged—white tiled walls, checkered flooring, mirror lined walls, servers dressed in tuxedos, an unparalleled atmosphere. There is nothing so glorious as spending a Friday afternoon lunch, lingering over cocktails, letting that turn into dinner. It is a New Orleans restaurant rite of passage. Among the more recent of Galatoire's brilliant additions, beyond opening the upstairs rooms (where reservations are honored), was the relatively recent hiring of Executive Chef Phillip Lopez. Galatoire's has long had great chefs running the kitchens, and Chef Phillip brings something new and special to the situation. He is not a native New Orleanian, though his is a fully embedded transplant and he is brimming with personality to match his talent. Talkative and smart, a front-and-center character perfect for Galatoire's lively vibe. The food, remains for better, what it is, old school classics. That said, there is a freshness popping from the platters of soufflé potatoes, tangy shrimp remoulade, comforting, crispy and garlicky Chicken Clemenceau, trout draped in lemony meunière sauce or beurre blanc, topped with lump crabmeat. It's all very familiar, some might even say fusty, but New Orleanians say, "Bring it on." Chef Phillip honors the tradition magnificently, thank you. And though some things have changed (ownership is a blend of old line and new guard), some things stay the same. Tradition #47: "Regulars just put it on their tab."

GALATOIRE'S OYSTERS ROCKEFELLER
(SERVES 12)

Over the years, many of the New Orleans' institutions have developed their own variations on the rich, herbaceous dish that was originally created in the city in 1899 by chef and restaurateur Jules Alciatore that was named for the wealthy and unforgettable John D. Rockefeller. Like Rockefeller's philanthropic legacy, the timeless dish named for him lives on through the ages.

If you must cook the oysters in batches, the rock salt will help to retain the heat within the first batches while the other batches cook. If Herbsaint is unavailable in your area, you may substitute Pernod. This dish can also be prepared with other types of shellfish, if absolutely necessary.

¾ cup chopped fennel (bulb only)

¼ cup chopped leeks (green and white parts)

¼ cup finely chopped curly parsley

¼ cup finely chopped scallions
(green and white parts)

¼ cup chopped celery

¼ cup ketchup

1½ cups cooked and drained chopped frozen spinach

½ teaspoon salt

½ teaspoon freshly ground white pepper

½ teaspoon cayenne pepper

1 teaspoon dried thyme leaves

1 teaspoon ground anise

2 teaspoon Worcestershire sauce

¼ cup Herbsaint liqueur

1 cup (2 sticks) melted salted butter

½ cup seasoned dried bread crumbs

12 cup rock salt

6 dozen oysters on the half shell

12 lemon wedges

Preheat the oven to 350°F.

To make the sauce, in a food processor combine the fennel, leeks, parsley, scallions, celery, ketchup, spinach, salt, white pepper, cayenne, thyme, anise, Worcestershire, and Herbsaint. Puree the mixture

thoroughly. Using a rubber spatula, scrape the contents of the food processor into a large mixing bowl. Stir in the butter and bread crumbs. Ensure that the mixture is well blended. Pour enough rock salt into twelve 8-inch cake pans to cover the bottom of the pans. Arrange 6 oysters in their half shells in each pan.

Fill a pastry bag with the Rockefeller sauce and pipe equal portions of the sauce over each shell. You may also use a tablespoon to distribute the sauce. Place the pans in the oven and bake for 5 minutes, or until the sauce sets. Turn the heat up to broil and broil the oysters for an additional 3–4 minutes, until the tops are bubbling.

Line each of 12 dinner plates with cloth napkins that have been folded into neat squares. Carefully nestle the pans of oysters within the folded napkins. Garnish with lemon wedges and serve at once.

CAFE BRULOT

(SERVES 6)

1 orange

1 lemon

12 whole cloves

3 cinnamon sticks

2 ounces brandy

2 ounces orange liqueur, such as Grand Marnier

2 tablespoons sugar

6 cups brewed French roast coffee, kept hot

Carefully carve the peel from the orange in a continuous coil fashion. Cut the lemon peel into ¼ inch curls and set aside. (see note). Stud the orange peel with the cloves, and spear one end of the coil with the fork. Set aside. Reserve the flesh of the orange and lemon for another use.

In a small saucepan, combine lemon peel, cinnamon sticks, liqueurs, and sugar over low heat until very warm to allow the ingredients to marry. The warmth is also required to ignite the brulot; cold liqueur will not flame. Once the ingredients are heated, pour them into a brulot bowl or a stainless steel bowl that has a flat bottom. Ignite the liqueur by holding a match to a ladle full of the liqueur. Once the ladle is lit, slowly lower it to the liqueur in the bowl. Hold the fork with the dangling clove-studded orange coil over the ignited bowl. Take extreme care not to burn yourself. Stir the flaming the liqueur with the ladle and ladle the liqueur over the orange coil you are holding over the bowl. The flame will spiral down the coil of orange peel and cloves, back into the bowl. Once you have poured the flaming liqueur down the coil several times to incorporate those flavors, remove the coil from the fork and put it in

the bowl. Slowly pour in the coffee while stirring to extinguish the flame. Ladle small amounts of the aeromantic coffee mixture into demitasse cups.

*Note: While it will not make as striking a presentation, an option for the home cook is to simply cut the peel from the citrus fruits and remove the pith instead of cutting the peels into elaborate coils. The pieces of orange peel can then be studded with the cloves.

COMPANY BURGER

4600 Freret Street
(504) 267-0320
thecompanyburger.com

Young and full of "piss and vinegar," Chef Adam Biderman applied skills learned during his time cooking at Atlanta's Holeman & Finch, to return home to New Orleans and open the Company Burger in 2011. He launched his burger joint with a plan to do "the best burger, my way," and that meant no lettuce or tomato. "Nothing's better than good meat, American cheese, and an excellent bun," he preached and preached and preached. Adam stuck to his guns, and the bold move paid off—he routinely sells out. Today diners can get a slice of tomato on their burger, as long as tomatoes are in season. That is Adam's mantra: it has to make sense and be in season to be on the menu—or on the burger. In fact, there are a lot of seasonal vegetable offerings, salads, or sides to go with the juicy beef, turkey, or lamb patties. There are cocktails, milkshakes, and always something sweet, fresh and new, making return visits a "must." Company Burger's original location sits on a stretch of Freret Street that has become quite a dining destination and Adam's place is certainly an important and vigorous part of the scene. He now has a second location in the newish South Market district near "The Dome." Here, diners can sit at the bar for full-service (versus counter service) on food, while sipping away on one of the clever batched cocktails "on tap." Adam

sharing a vegetable side dish for this book was his way of being the smart-ass that he is. He is well loved for just that kind of attitude and a killer burger.

LOCAL CORN & CHERRY TOMATO SALAD

(SERVES 6–8)

8 ears corn, preferably yellow sweet, in the husk

3 pints cherry tomatoes, ideally yellow, red, and black

3 bunches fresh basil, washed and shredded into chiffonade

4 bunches green onion, thinly sliced

3 cloves fresh garlic, minced

3 tablespoons celery seed

2 tablespoons honey

Salt and pepper

2 cups cider vinegar

1½ cups extra virgin olive oil

To prepare the corn: Heat oven to 350°F and cook corn in the husk until your kitchen smells like roasting corn, about 30–45 minutes.

Cool the corn and, after 15 minutes, start shucking. The silk will have steamed out of the ears and will come out clean. Brush any remaining hairs off with a towel. Cut the corn off the cob using a sharp knife. Placing the corn in a large bowl or baking dish helps keep all the kernels from flying everywhere. Hold the corncob vertically, applying pressure to the top of the cob so you don't lose it. With a mandoline, this job is significantly easier, but make sure that you have set the opening wide enough to get the whole kernels.

To assemble the salad: Wash the tomatoes and cut them in half. Set aside.

Combine the corn, basil, green onions, garlic, celery seed, and honey, and season lightly with salt and pepper.

Add half of the vinegar and oil and mix. Adjust seasoning to taste (I like heavy pepper). Add remaining vinegar and oil, mix, and toss in tomatoes at the end. Adjust seasoning or vinegar, depending how tart you want it. Ideally the salad should be balanced, like a vinaigrette. Let the salad stand in the refrigerator at least 4 hours before serving. Cold is good, room temperature is better.

CREOLE CREAMERY

4924 Prytania Street
(504) 894-8680
creolecreamery.com

Tucked inside the former and legendary McKenzie's Bakery building on Prytania Street, David Bergeron and Bryan Gilmore spin artisan ice creams and sorbets, in a traditional American ice cream parlor setting. The best part is the creative flavors that span from Red Velvet, Lavender Honey, or Cucumber Dill to I Scream Fudge!, White Chocolate–Peanut Butter Pie, and many, many more. They do seasonal flavors like Christmas Morning, and every now and then there is homage to McKenzie's Bakery or other food icons like Hubig's Apple Pie. The shop is always buzzing, and they are often featured on the Food Network. This recipe combines the licorice-like flavor of Herbsaint, an anise-flavored liqueur that gives the ice cream its green color, with zesty orange and rich dark chocolate. Very New Orleans.

GREEN FAIRY ICE CREAM

(MAKES ABOUT 2 QUARTS)

¾ cup sugar

5 large egg yolks

3 cups half-and-half

1 cup heavy cream

Pinch of salt

½ cup Herbsaint

¼ teaspoon pure vanilla extract

½ cup dark chocolate (we use Valrhona), chopped

½ cup candied orange peel, cut into ¼-inch cubes

Mix the sugar and egg yolks together in a bowl with a whisk. Meanwhile, heat the half-and-half, cream, and salt in a saucepan. Don't boil it; just heat it to a light simmer. Then pour it slowly into the egg-sugar mixture, whisking as you do it.

Pour it all into the saucepan and cook over low heat, stirring, until it has thickened enough that it will coat the back of a spoon, 8–10 minutes. Remove from heat and let cool. Cover with plastic wrap so no skin forms, and put in the refrigerator for a few hours.

When chilled, add Herbsaint and vanilla. Process the mixture in an ice cream maker until frozen to soft-serve consistency, about 20–30 minutes. Remove from ice cream maker into a metal or glass container, and fold in the chocolate and orange peel. Cover again with plastic wrap or wax paper, and store in freezer for 6–8 hours.

HAYDEL'S BAKE SHOP

3117 Magazine Street
(504) 267-3165
haydelbakery.com

Haydel is a name synonymous with local sweet treat specialties like petit fours, pecan and chocolate-topped turtles and king cakes (the round pastry served during Mardi Gras season) to name a scant few. In the Garden District, on Magazine Street, Ryan Haydel recently opened a petite version of the family bakery. Here, the cases are filled with all sorts of cakes, cookies, fruit cakes, pralines and other baked goods. I was excited when he offered me this traditional Russian Cake recipe. It is a lesser-known traditional cake with historical context and local "flavor" that mimics a cocktail. Shrouded in myth and local lore, the Haydel family prefers the story that this cake dates back to 1872 when the Grand Duke Alexis of Russia came to New Orleans for Mardi Gras.

RUSSIAN CAKE

(YIELDS 1 8-INCH CAKE)

8 cups almond cake scraps (crumbled, loosely packed)*

1 cup chocolate or devil's food cake scraps (crumbled, loosely packed)*

1 8-inch round yellow cake baked per box instructions

1¼ cup seedless raspberry jelly plus ¼ more for construction

2 tablespoons rum or 1 tablespoon plus 1 teaspoon rum flavor (no alcohol)

¼ teaspoon anise oil or anise extract

¼ cup plus 1 tablespoon Simple Syrup (equal parts sugar and water)

Buttercream or white icing

Sprinkles

* Bake a white sheet cake per box instructions and flavor with 1 tablespoon almond extract

* Bake your favorite chocolate or devil's food cake from box or scratch

Mix your favorite yellow cake from a box or scratch and bake (1) 8-inch round cake based on the recipe's instructions and let cool. Once cool, slice the cake crosswise into 3 thin, equal layers. Save two layers for the construction of the cake and crumble the remaining layer. It is ok to have bigger and smaller pieces of cake when crumbled.

In a large mixing bowl combine the Almond and Chocolate scraps and add the crumbled yellow cake.

In a smaller bowl, mix together the jelly, rum flavor, anise flavor and simple syrup with a whisk until combined.

Add the liquid ingredients to the cake scraps and mix together by hand. You are looking to wet and combine the ingredients, not to smash up the cake too much. You want a few large pieces of cake to remain. (It will look like raw ground meat when ready).

To construct the cake: Layer an 8" cake pan with parchment. Place one 8-inch round yellow thin layer

down in the pan. Smear 2 tablespoons raspberry jelly to cover the entire layer. Take your cake mixture and pack tightly on top of the cake layer. Cover with remaining 2 tablespoons of raspberry jelly and top with the second yellow cake layer. Cover with a piece of parchment paper and press down firmly on the cake, packing it down as much as possible. For desired results, place an 8" round cake board on the top of the cake and place a weight (brick, books, etc. . . .) on top and leave for 1 hour. Once the weight has been removed, refrigerate for at least 2 hours.

Remove the top piece of parchment paper, and turn out on an 8-inch cake board, or a platter. Remove the remaining parchment from around the cake.

Top with a ¼-inch layer of white icing or buttercream of your choice.

Refrigerate for up to 4 days. Add sprinkles to top when ready to serve.

HOBNOBBER CAFE

W. Metairie Avenue
(504) 734-8488
hobnobbercafe.com

Executive chefs and owners Troy, Cindy and Ryan (their son) Timphony are a culinary imperative. They are a quintessential New Orleans Italian family with deep restaurant and ancestral roots. Almost everyone in the family contributes to this restaurant and their customers are considered their extended family. When you think of "mom and pop" places, Hobnobber is the very definition. The menu is filled with plate lunch favorites from pastas to poboys, soups and salads. Daily specials change weekly and some of the more popular include their trout amandine, paneed veal, artichoke chicken, stuffed shells, meatballs, hamburger steak, meatloaf . . . I could go on. Around the third week of March, many locals celebrate the Feast of St. Joseph, the patron Saint of famine. It is customary to bake cookies for elaborately decorating private (home) or Church altars, and those who open their doors for people to view the altars, also serve a meal. The Timphony family does such a meal from their restaurant and this is their take on the holy day.

"The Feast of St. Joseph—Italians prepare this feast to give thanks to St. Joseph, which many regard as the Patron Saint of Italians, for preventing a famine during the Middle Ages. According to legend, there was a severe drought at the time, and the people prayed for their patron saint to bring them rain. They promised that if God answered their prayers through Joseph's intercession, they would prepare a large feast to honor him. The rain did come, and the people of Sicily prepared a large banquet for their patron saint. The fava bean was the crop which saved the population from starvation and is a traditional part of Saint Joseph's Day altars and traditions.

So help us celebrate St. Joseph and join in the feast that will include Bucatini pasta with Milanese gravy, fried catfish, paneed eggplant, stuffed bread, salad, homemade cookies and a blessed lucky (fava) bean"

PASTA MILANESE

(MAKES 1 GALLON)

2 cups chopped onion

2 cups chopped fennel bulb (save the leaves for later use)

4 cloves garlic chopped fine

3 cups tomato paste

12 cups tomato sauce

1 cup chopped fine fennel leaves (leaves from fennel bulb used earlier)

4 ounces toasted pine nuts

2 cups chopped sardines

½ cup chopped flat parsley

¼ cup olive oil

¼ cup sugar

¼ cup dried sweet basil

1 tablespoon salt

1 tablespoon black pepper

1 tablespoon Tony's Cajun seasoning

1 teaspoon cracked red pepper

In a thick bottom pot on medium to high heat, sauté

onion, fennel, garlic in olive oil for 5 minutes or until onions become translucent but do not let them burn. Add tomato paste, sauté for about 5 minutes, stir frequently so that sauce does not stick to the bottom of pan. Add tomato sauce, use tomato sauce cans to fill with water and add to paste.

Add salt, pepper, sugar, garlic, Tony's, basil, cracked red pepper and bring to a boil for 5 more minutes. Stir frequently.

Lower heat to a simmer. Add parsley, chopped fennel, toasted pine nuts and sardines. Let gravy simmer for 2 hours on low heat.

Traditionally this sauce is served with a fat, tube-like pasta called bucatini. To accompany the dish at Hobnobber Café we serve it with fried crispy catfish (photo above), panned eggplant medallions and hot, buttery bread.

ITALIAN FIG COOKIES

For the dough:

4 cups unbleached all-purpose flour

1 and ½ tablespoons baking powder

¼ teaspoon salt

½ cup sugar

1 cup vegetable shortening

1 large egg

1 tablespoon pure vanilla extract

½ cup milk

For the fig filling:

1 cup dried fig

1 cup dried dates

¾ cup raisins

¼ cup honey

½ teaspoon cinnamon

¼ cup orange marmalade

½ cup walnuts

For the icing:

2 cups confectioners' sugar

Water or condensed milk (to consistency desired)

Directions for preparing cookie dough: Sift flour, baking powder and salt into a large bowl. Add sugar and stir well. Cut in the shortening with a fork or pastry blender and work the mixture until it looks like corn meal. In a separate bowl beat egg, vanilla and milk together.

Add the egg mixture to the flour mixture and knead the dough for five minutes on a floured surface. The dough will be a soft texture. Divide the dough into four pieces and wrap each piece in plastic wrap.

Refrigerate the dough for 45 minutes.

Directions for filling: With a food processor grind the figs, dates, and raisins until coarse. Add remaining filling ingredients and mix well. The mixture will be thick and sticky. Set aside and let stand. Take plastic storage bags and fill with portions of the fig filling. Close tightly and snip one end so that mixture will squeeze out in a small log like fashion. You can also use a pastry bag without the tip on.

Making the cookies: Remove one portion of dough at a time from refrigerator to work with. On a floured surface roll the dough into a 12 inch square. Cut dough into 4 3- inch rectangle pieces. Pipe filling from bags down the middle of the dough. Carefully fold over dough and pinch the edges to cover the fig filling inside. With flour on your hands, roll the dough until it becomes a long half inch round piece of dough. Cut dough into 2 inch pieces and make 3 tiny diagonal slits on the top of each cookie with a sharp knife. Place each cookie on a baking sheet, lined with parchment paper, making sure to leave 1–2 inches between each cookie. Bake for 12–15 minutes or until cookies are golden in color. Remove cookies from oven and transfer to wire rack to cool.

For the icing: Place confectioners' sugar in a bowl. Add a small amount of water or milk until sugar is a smooth consistency but not runny. Add a touch of food coloring, your choice, to icing and mix until color is to your liking. Carefully dip the tops of each cookie into the icing. Sprinkle the tops of each cookie with colored sprinkles immediately after icing. Let icing dry completely before storing in airtight container. Enjoy!

HIGH HAT

4500 Freret Street
(504) 754.1336
highhatcafe.com

Chef Adolfo Garcia is a very well-liked chef in New Orleans. His culinary prowess goes way back, but he is best known for opening RioMar (seafood), then La Boca (meat-centric), Ancora (Neapolitan-style pizza) and High Hat (southern inspired). He and his restaurants are very popular. With his business partner Chip Apperson these guys showcase mad love for southern food, and the menu fairly is ring-the-dinner-bell delicious. Their tag line, "The Delta comes to the Bayou," says it all.

STEWED CHICKEN WITH MUSTARD GREENS & SPOON BREAD
(SERVES 4)

Stewed chicken is a classic southern dish that can be found cooking on the stove at Grandma's house on any Sunday afternoon. It is usually pretty heavy, and an after-lunch nap is almost required. This version is made lighter with the addition of lemon juice and fresh herbs. To help cut through some of the richness, it is best served with vinegary braised greens and spoon bread. The greens help to round out the dish without making you sleepy, and the spoon bread soaks up the delicious gravy dripping off the chicken without being as filling as a traditional bread or steamed rice.

For the chicken:

1 chicken, quartered, backbone removed

Salt and pepper

Soybean oil, up to ½ cup

½ cup flour

⅔ cup diced yellow onion

⅓ cup diced celery

⅓ cup diced bell pepper

3 cloves garlic, minced

½ teaspoon cayenne pepper

1 quart chicken stock

1 bunch fresh thyme

1 tablespoon sliced green onions

1 tablespoon chopped parsley

1 teaspoon hot sauce, or to taste

½ teaspoon lemon juice, or to taste

For the mustard greens:

2 yellow onions, sliced

1 tablespoon chopped garlic

½ cup bacon pieces

1 ham hock

¼ cup light brown sugar

½ teaspoon crushed red pepper

1 pint Abita amber beer

4 tablespoons red wine vinegar, divided

1 pint chicken stock

5 bunches mustard greens, chopped

Salt and pepper to taste

For the spoon bread:

1 quart whole milk

¾ cup coarse yellow cornmeal

¼ cup yellow corn flour

2 tablespoons unsalted butter

1½ teaspoons salt

4 egg yolks

4 egg whites

To make the chicken: Season chicken pieces with salt and pepper. Heat a large cast iron pan over medium-high heat and coat with oil. Cook chicken, skin side down, in batches until the skin is turning brown and crispy. Set chicken aside.

Pour oil and chicken fat from pan into a measuring container and add enough oil to make ½ cup. Return oil to pan and heat until almost smoking. Whisk in flour and cook over medium heat, stirring constantly, until the roux turns the color of milk chocolate. Turn off the heat and add onions, celery, bell pepper, garlic, and cayenne. Stir until well mixed. Set aside.

In a large pot bring chicken stock to a boil. Carefully mix in the roux and whisk until incorporated. Turn down heat and simmer for ten minutes, skimming any fat that rises to the surface.

Preheat oven to 350°F. Place chicken pieces in a roasting pan. Tie fresh thyme with butcher's twine and add to pan. Pour in enough of the thickened stock to cover everything. Cover roasting pan with parchment paper and foil, then place in oven for 3 hours, or until the chicken reaches an internal temperature of 175°F. Remove from oven and uncover. Let the chicken cool in the liquid for at least 3 hours or overnight.

Remove the chicken from the braising liquid and set aside. Put all of the liquid into a large pot and reduce by one-third, skimming any fat that rises.

Transfer to a smaller pot and keep warm on the stove.

To make the mustard greens: In a large pot, sweat onions, garlic, bacon, and ham hocks. Add brown sugar and red pepper and cook until sugar is starting to caramelize. Pour in beer, 2 tablespoons vinegar, and stock and bring to a boil. Add greens and cook until tender, then season with salt, pepper, and the remaining 2 tablespoons vinegar.

To make the spoon bread: Preheat oven to 400°F. Grease a 9 x 9-inch baking pan.

Bring the milk up to a boil and whisk in the cornmeal and corn flour. Cook over medium-high heat for about 5 minutes, stirring constantly. Add the butter and salt and remove from the heat. Whisk in the egg yolks one at a time. Beat the egg whites until they hold medium peaks, and fold them into the hot batter. Pour into the greased baking pan and bake uncovered for 30–45 minutes. It should rise considerably and be golden brown on top, but will not seem set. Remove from the oven and let stand in a warm area for 10 minutes to firm up, and then serve immediately.

To finish the dish: Heat a 12-inch skillet and add the cooked chicken, skin side down. Cover with the braising liquid and bring to a boil. Turn down to a simmer, cover, and cook until the chicken is warmed through and starting to fall off the bone. Carefully remove and set one chicken quarter on each of four serving plates. To the sauce add the green onions, parsley, hot sauce, and lemon juice, and taste for seasoning. Spoon sauce over chicken and serve with a large spoonful of mustard greens and a large spoonful of spoon bread.

BLUEBERRY CANE SYRUP PIE IN A CORNMEAL CRUST

(SERVES 8)

For the crust:

2¼ cups all-purpose flour

½ cup coarse yellow cornmeal

2 tablespoons sugar

1 teaspoon kosher salt

½ stick unsalted butter

½ cup lard

½ cup buttermilk

For the filling:

4½ cups fresh blueberries

⅓ cup cane syrup

3 tablespoon sugar

7 teaspoons cornstarch

5 teaspoons lemon juice

Pinch of ground cinnamon

Put the dry ingredients for the crust into a food processor. Pulse six times. Scatter the butter and lard over dry mix and pulse ten times. Slowly pour in buttermilk while pulsing twelve more times.

Move dough to a mixing bowl and knead a few times until a ball forms. Separate into two-thirds and one-third, and form into disks. Wrap disks separately and place in refrigerator for at least 15 minutes, or overnight.

Remove larger disk from fridge and let sit at room temperature for 15 minutes.

Roll out large disk, fit it into a 10-inch pie pan, and place back in fridge.

Preheat oven to 400°F. Remove smaller dough disk from fridge and let sit for 15 minutes. Meanwhile, mix filling ingredients in a large bowl and let sit for 10 minutes. Pour filling into chilled pie shell.

Roll out smaller crust until large enough to cover pie. Using your fingers, dab outside rim of bottom crust with water and cover with top crust, pressing together with a fork to seal. Trim the excess crust off with a small knife and cut vents into the top crust. Bake at 400°F for 30 minutes. Rotate the pie and bake for another 30 minutes at 350°F, or until juice is slowly bubbling through the vent holes.

Remove from oven and let cool for 2 hours before serving. Serve warm with fresh whipped cream and peach ice cream.

LA PETITE GROCERY

4238 Magazine Street
(504) 891-3377
lapetitegrocery.com

Justin Devillier, a James Beard Award-winning executive chef, and his wife Mia Freiberger-Devillier, run this comfortably stylish restaurant two years ago, infusing it with Chef Justin's love for unique ingredients, locally sourced and sometimes even hand grown. The menu has a bistro vibration and the food is both smart and sexy. There is a bar area with seating for those who want a properly made cocktail and a bite, or you can step into the main dining room for the full experience. Sunday brunch is soothing, and the outdoor seating is great for watching Magazine Street's bustle. Some pop in to La Petite Grocery for a cocktail and dessert in the charming bar area.

TAGLIATELLE WITH GULF SHRIMP & FIELD PEAS

Chef Justin loves local seafood and he loves making pasta. Both are incredible when combined with the earthiness of field peas and heady aged Parmesan.

(SERVES 4)

2 tablespoons salt

1 pound fresh Gulf shrimp, preferably 12-count

½ cup cooked black-eyed peas

½ cup cooked soybeans

5 ounces salt, divided 1 ounce and 4 ounces

12 ounces fresh tagliatelle

2 ounces unsalted butter

Salt to taste

1 teaspoon white pepper

2 tablespoons snipped chives

2 ounces lemon juice

1 tablespoon picked oregano

8 grams shaved *Piave vecchio* or aged Parmesan

Fill a large pot with 8–10 quarts of water, add

2 tablespoons salt, and bring to a boil. Meanwhile, place ¼ cup water in a large saucepan and bring to a simmer. Add the shrimp and gently cook through. Add the peas and beans to warm.

To the large pot of water add the pasta and cook until al dente, about 5–10 minutes, tasting frequently after the first 2 minutes. Drain and keep warm.

In the pan with the shrimp, peas, and beans, gently swirl in the butter over low heat. Place the pasta in the pan with the shrimp-peas-butter sauce and season with salt to taste, pepper, chives, and lemon juice. Serve garnished with oregano and shaved cheese.

BUTTERSCOTCH PUDDING

La Petite's version of butterscotch pudding returns the dessert to its southern roots, incorporating Louisiana cane syrup and New Orleans rum, and serves it with toasted pecan madeleines.

(SERVES 6-8)

3 ounces butter

1 tablespoon Steen's cane syrup or molasses

½ pound dark brown sugar

3 tablespoons amber or dark rum

½ teaspoon salt, or more to taste

4¼ cups cream

1 vanilla bean

¾ cup plus 2 tablespoons granulated sugar

3 sheets gelatin or 1 tablespoon gelatin powder

6 egg yolks

Special equipment: pastry brush

Melt butter with cane syrup. Add brown sugar, rum, and salt and cook over medium heat until bubbling and just beginning to smoke. Add 4 cups cream and whisk until caramel is dissolved. Scrape seeds out of vanilla bean and add both seeds and bean to cream mixture. Cover and allow to steep.

Meanwhile, combine granulated sugar and ¼ cup water in a heavy-bottomed, nonreactive pot. Cover and bring to a boil. When steam begins to escape, remove the lid. Allow sugar to caramelize to a deep amber, brushing down sides of pot frequently to prevent crystallization. Once caramel is ready, immediately take it off the heat and whisk in the remaining ¼ cup cream. Add this caramel mixture to cream mixture, whisk thoroughly, and gently warm until caramel is totally dissolved.

At this point, begin to bloom gelatin by submerging sheets in ice water (if using powdered gelatin, follow manufacturer's instructions). Then temper some of the warm caramel-cream mixture into the yolks, return yolk mix to the pot, and cook until the pudding is the texture of a thick crème anglaise. Immediately whisk in bloomed gelatin and strain mixture into a bowl set over ice. Allow to cool until moderately thickened before portioning into small,

wide-mouthed mason jars or other decorative containers. Allow to set for at least 4 hours.

Serve with gently whipped cream and cookies.

HEARD DAT KITCHEN

2520 Felicity Street
(504) 510-4248
hearddatkitchen.com

Chef Jeffrey Heard and family own and operate their neighborhood restaurant serving classic Creole soul food. It's all-hands-on-deck meaning everyone, his wife, children and grandchildren are involved in some way. Originally a to-go only restaurant with some outdoor seating, there is now a small indoor dining area. Chef Jeff made his bones as a banquet chef at white tablecloth Restaurant August. "I learned a lot there," he tells me, "I put a lot of what I learned combined with my own tastes into my dishes." And Chef Jeff also takes input from his kids, one of who dubbed the sweet-spicy barbecue sauced wings, "skeesh"—a word that they tell me is similar to "aloha" with multiple meanings. Those "Skeesh" wings are fantastic, as is the blackened fish dish with lobster potatoes and lobster sauce, called "Superdome." One of my favorite meals here is Gumbo Combo—file gumbo with rice, a side of potato salad and a grilled cheese sandwich. For those who don't know, grilled cheese and gumbo is a school cafeteria staple.

NEW ORLEANS STYLE BARBECUED SHRIMP
(SERVES 2)

6 large shrimp (heads and shells on)

2 teaspoons of Creole/Cajun seasoning

2 teaspoons of salt

3 teaspoon of black pepper, divided.

1 tablespoon of minced garlic

1 tablespoon of dried parsley

½ teaspoon of rosemary

1 teaspoon of Worcestershire sauce

1 stick of butter

⅓ cup of beer

Sauté shrimp for 1 minute. Add the salt, Creole/Cajun seasoning and 1 teaspoon of black pepper. Stir to combine. Add 2 tablespoons of butter, garlic, parsley, rosemary and Worcestershire sauce. Stir to coat shrimp. Add 2 more tablespoons of butter and simmer for one minute. Add ¼ cup of beer, stir and cook for another minute or 2. Finish with ½ stick of butter and remaining 2 teaspoons of black pepper.

Serve with lots of crusty French bread to soak up the sauce.

CRAWFISH ORZO PASTA

(SERVES 4)

Four cups of orzo

Water for boiling

For the pasta cream sauce:

4 cups of water

4 cups of heavy cream

1 tablespoon of black pepper

1 teaspoon of red pepper (cayenne)

2 tablespoons of chicken base

1 tablespoon of basil

6 cloves of minced garlic

2 cups of corn

For the crawfish tail "marinade":

12 or 16 ounces peeled crawfish tails

¼ pound of butter

1 tablespoon of black pepper

1 teaspoon of red pepper

1 tablespoon of granulated garlic

1 teaspoon of salt

1 tablespoon of basil

To serve:

½ stick of butter

Boil the pasta: Boil 8 cups of water. Add 4 cups of orzo. Boil for 4 minutes, drain and set aside.

To prepare the pasta sauce: Combine all ingredients, except for the corn, and bring to a boil. Reduce temperature half way. Add 2 cups of corn, stir and set aside.

For the crawfish tail "marinade": Combine all together and simmer until butter melts.

To assemble: Combine the marinated crawfish tails with the cream sauce, and stir in orzo. Add a ½ stick of butter, reduce heat and stir gently. Serve warm.

PATOIS

6078 Laurel Street
(504) 895-9441
patoisnola.com

Tucked away in a predominantly residential neighborhood near Audubon Park, Chef Aaron Burgau has created a chic French restaurant with a New Orleans accent. Often highly visible at the farmers markets, Chefs Aaron Burgau and Jonathan Lomonaco are big supporters of local community gardens and ingredients from nearby farms. The menu changes weekly to reflect what's available, and there is always something fun and different to try on the menu. Patois' pastry is the handiwork of Lisa Alessandro, who takes her cues from relevant flavors of the moment and seasonal fruits. There is also a clever cocktail program with fresh and lively drinks, classic in foundation, and tweaked to be current. Chef Aaron sums it up: "This is a fun place to dine and drink."

LAMB RIBS
(SERVES 2–4 AS APPETIZER)

For the lamb rib rub:

4 tablespoons cumin seed

4 tablespoons fennel seed

4 tablespoons coriander seed

1 cup granulated onion

1 cup granulated garlic

2 teaspoons cayenne

4 tablespoons smoked paprika

2 cups raw sugar

1 cup black pepper

2 cups salt

4 teaspoons allspice

4 teaspoons dry mustard

For the lamb:

1 rack lamb ribs (6–8 ribs)

4 tablespoons lamb rib rub

For the green tomato jam:

5 pounds green tomatoes, diced

2 cups apple cider vinegar

2 cups sugar

2 tablespoons salt

2 tablespoons pickling spice

1 cup onion, diced

1 teaspoon crushed red pepper

2 cloves

½ cinnamon stick

To make the rub: In a nonstick pan, toast cumin, fennel, and coriander seeds. Grind in a spice grinder or mortar and pestle. Combine remaining ingredients and set aside or store in an airtight container until ready to use.

To cook the lamb: Rub lamb ribs with the lamb rib rub. On an outdoor grill/smoker or in a home oven, set temperature to 225°F and cook ribs for about 4

hours, until meat is tender and almost falls off the bones.

To make the jam: In a large stockpot, combine all ingredients and cook for 30–40 minutes or until thick.

To plate: When ribs are finished cooking, let them rest, covered lightly, for 10–15 minutes, then cut the rack into individual ribs. On a serving plank, place three sets of two ribs stacked crisscross and topped with a generous tablespoon or two of green tomato jam. Serve immediately.

CREOLE CREAM CHEESE SEMIFREDDO

(SERVES 12-15)

12 ounces cream

12 ounces Creole cream cheese

4 yolks

7 ounces sugar, divided

4 egg whites

Whip cream to medium peaks. Run Creole cream cheese through a blender until smooth; fold into whipped cream. Whip yolks and 3 ounces sugar until thick and pale; fold into dairy mixture. Whip egg whites with remaining 4 ounces sugar to form medium-stiff peaks; fold into dairy-yolk mixture. Scoop into fleximold, and smooth the surface. Freeze about 4 hours, or until firm. Unmold and serve.

BLUEBERRY COMPOTE

(MAKES SLIGHTLY MORE THAN 1 PINT)

1½ heaping quarts fresh or frozen blueberries

1½ ounces sugar

2 tablespoons lemon juice

2 (3-inch) cinnamon sticks

Combine all ingredients. Boil for 7–8 minutes, or until berries begin to pop. Cool to room temperature to serve.

LEMON—POPPY SEED SHORTBREAD

(MAKES 2 DOZEN)

8 ounces softened butter

Zest of 2 lemons

½ teaspoon lemon oil

½ cup sugar

2 cups all-purpose flour

1 tablespoon poppy seeds

Cream butter, lemon zest, lemon oil, and sugar. Slowly add flour until combined. Stir in poppy seeds.

Roll into logs and refrigerate until firm.

Preheat oven to 350°F. Slice dough logs into ¼-inch slices and place on ungreased cookie sheets. Bake for 10 minutes, turning cookie sheets halfway through baking. Cool shortbread on sheets for five minutes, then on wire racks.

ST. JAMES CHEESE COMPANY

5004 Prytania Street
(504) 899-4737
641 Tchoupitoulas Street
(504) 304-1485
stjamescheese.com

Step through the front door to either location of this busy cheese shop and breathe deep. The heavenly scent of washed rinds, fresh and aging cheeses, blend gorgeously with cured meats, yeasty bread, olives, and other condiments. Richard and Danielle Sutton run the show here and were among those who opened soon after the storm, in 2006. Their pedigree in cheese-mongering is impeccable, and their love for the city unwavering. They offer cheese classes, hold interesting pairing events (Cocktails and Curds), support local vendors and purveyors, and in short have become essential. Almost every restaurant of note seeks their advice and buys the cheeses they source. Richard and Danielle also offer a wide menu of hot and cold sandwiches, salads, cheese and meat boards—and then there is the obvious, a rich, melty mac and cheese, which they've shared here.

PEPATO MACARONI & CHEESE

This is a very easy and fast mac and cheese recipe, but it also has a lot of complexity. If you can't find pecorino pepato, substitute another pecorino and use a generous amount of freshly ground black pepper.

(SERVES 4-6)

1 stick unsalted butter

½ cup flour

1 large shallot, finely diced

¾ cup white wine

3 cups whole milk

3 cups grated pecorino pepato

1 pound cooked macaroni

Melt butter over medium heat. Whisk in flour and stir for 2 minutes until it smells nutty. Add diced shallots and cook for 1 minute. Whisk in white wine and stir until mixture is smooth. Slowly pour in milk while whisking to make a smooth sauce. Add grated cheese, a bit at a time, and stir until it is completely melted. If the sauce is too thick, you can thin it with a little more milk. You can mix this right away with hot cooked pasta, or refrigerate the sauce for later. It heats up and melts really well on the stovetop or in the microwave.

ALABAMA PEACH CHUTNEY

This chutney is delicious served with cheese or cold meats, on sandwiches, or used as a glaze on a pork roast. It is a great way to avoid throwing out overripe peaches, from a rash moment at the farmers market when you spied them piled beautifully on the table and bought way too many.

(MAKES 4 LARGE OR 8 SMALL JARS)

30 ripe peaches

5 cups cider vinegar

5 cups sugar

3 teaspoons salt

3 white onions, finely chopped

3 cloves garlic, finely chopped

2 tablespoons mustard seeds

2 cups golden raisins

Blanch peaches in boiling water for 3 minutes. Remove and let cool. Peel the peaches and cut fruit away from the pit, chopping it roughly in large chunks.

Combine cider vinegar, sugar, and salt in a large pot and bring to a boil. Add onions and garlic and cook for 5 minutes. Add peaches, mustard seeds, and raisins to the pot and boil for 30 minutes. Reduce heat and simmer for 2 hours.

Prepare and sterilize canning jars. Bring the chutney back up to a boil before removing from heat. Ladle into sterilized jars and add rings and lids. The heat from the chutney will seal the jars. Set on a wire rack to cool.

TACEAUX LOCEAUX

737 Octavia Street
(504) 336-3656
@TLNola

Maribeth and Alex Del Castillo are the chef-owners of the first New Orleans food truck of the "gourmet" kind. Taceaux Loceaux rocked their business with cleverly named, super-delicious "taceaux" like Messin' with Texas (slow-roasted brisket, shredded cabbage, radish, cilantro, crema, and onion on flour tortillas) or Jane Deaux (seasoned braised greens, potatoes, Cotija cheese, crema, salsa, cilantro, and toasted pepitas on corn tortillas). They are prolific users of social media, posting for both the truck and their brick-and-mortar restaurant. Chefs Mairbeth and Alex helped spearhead New Orleans's food truck movement and are considered local gurus in navigating the sometimes murky city rules. Their restaurant is bold and colorful like the truck and with an expanded menu of taceaux, salads and bowls. For the Gaudin annual St. Patrick's Day party, Taceaux Loceaux created the O'Taceaux of corned beef, cabbage, potatoes and horseradish cream. It's divine. For the book, Chefs Maribeth and Alex offer one of their "special" menu items that now has a place on the restaurant menu.

GULF CEVICHE

We love this recipe, as it really showcases the beautiful fish from the Gulf Coast. Amberjack, mahi mahi, and snapper are all excellent choices, as is shrimp if you prefer, but defer to your fishmonger's recommendations should those be unavailable in your area. You want the freshest fish you can find.

(SERVES 4)

For the ceviche:

1 pound firm-fleshed fish

Juice of 6 lemons

Juice of 6 limes

¼ cup apple cider vinegar

3 jalapeños, seeds removed, finely minced

5 garlic cloves, finely minced

1 bunch cilantro, chopped

2 teaspoons salt

For the charred jalapeño dressing:

2 jalapeños

3 cloves garlic

½ bunch cilantro, roughly chopped

½ cup sour cream

½ cup mayonnaise

2 tablespoons cider vinegar

Salt to taste

For assembly:

3 corn tortillas

Peanut oil, for frying

Salt

1 head butter lettuce or 8 corn tortillas

2 avocados

½ bunch cilantro, leaves only, for garnish

To make the ceviche: Cut the fish into uniform ½-inch dice. Combine with remaining seven ingredients in a large mixing bowl. Allow to marinate in refrigerator for at least 6 hours and preferably overnight, stirring occasionally.

To make the dressing: Roast jalapeños in oven until skin is blistered and charred. Cool. Remove skin and seeds. Combine all dressing ingredients in blender, and process until smooth. Refrigerate until ready to use.

To assemble: Julienne the 3 tortillas. Heat oil in a heavy-bottomed pot until thermometer registers between 350° and 365°F. Fry tortilla threads until crisp. Salt immediately after removing from oil.

Arrange 3 butter lettuce leaves or 2 corn tortillas on each of four plates. Slice the avocados and add 3 slices to each leaf. Portion ceviche onto each leaf, topping with 1 tablespoon jalapeño dressing. Garnish with fried tortilla threads and cilantro leaves.

TARTINE

7217 Perrier Street
(504) 866-4860
tartineneworleans.com

Chef-owner Cara Benson is a local gal with a dream and mission: to have "a little piece of Paris in the Black Pearl." Done and done. Nestled into a one-time frame shop abutting "Uptown Square" (the home of the Tuesday Crescent City Farmers Market), Cara and her team, including her husband Evan, bake crisp-crusted baguettes, chewy loaves of ciabatta, tender focaccia, and hearty wheat bread to hold slices of deli meats, creamy cheese, or the house special, slabs of rustic country paté, pickles, and house-made jams. The scones, brioche, and bagels are also lovely, and there is no skipping the airy yet rich and chocolatey mousse. Always keen to support local businesses, Cara buys much of her produce from the farmers market outside her door, to turn into soups or sandwich fillings. She was among the first to serve and sell locally roasted French Truck Coffees.

DUCK LIVER MOUSSE WITH PEACH–JALAPEÑO MARMALADE

(SERVES 10-12)

For the duck liver mousse:

1 pound duck livers (or chicken livers)

1 pound butter, at room temperature

2 shallots, finely diced

1 teaspoon chopped thyme

1 tablespoon salt

¼ teaspoon white pepper

⅛ teaspoon freshly ground nutmeg

⅛ teaspoon ground cloves

¼ cup cognac or other brandy

For the peach-jalapeño marmalade:

1 shallot, finely diced

2 jalapeños, seeds and pith removed, finely diced

1–3 tablespoons olive oil

4 peaches, peeled and diced

¼ cup sugar

2 tablespoons white balsamic vinegar

Salt and pepper, to taste

To make the mousse: Clean, wash, and dry duck livers.

Melt 2 tablespoons butter in a heavy sauté pan over medium-low heat. Sauté diced shallots and thyme until translucent, about 8 minutes. Add duck livers, salt, pepper, nutmeg, and cloves to the pan and cook, turning once, until livers have firmed and are pink on the inside, about 3–4 minutes. Remove duck livers and deglaze pan with cognac, then reduce liquid by half and remove from heat.

Transfer livers and liquid to food processor and puree until smooth and slightly cooled. With the machine running, add remaining softened butter a tablespoon at a time to form the mousse.

For the smoothest texture, press the mousse through a mesh sieve using a plastic spatula or a dough scraper.

Transfer finished mousse to an airtight container and cover surface with plastic wrap until ready to use.

To make the marmalade: Sauté shallots and jalapeños in olive oil. Add peaches. Season with sugar, vinegar, salt, and pepper. Bring mixture to a boil, reduce heat to a simmer, and cook until thickened.

DARK CHOCOLATE MOUSSE

(SERVES 6-8)

18 ounces dark chocolate

1 quart cream

9 egg yolks

1 egg

7 ounces sugar

Melt chocolate and keep warm. Whip cream to soft peaks. Beat yolks and egg. Cook sugar with enough water to cover until it reaches soft-ball stage (234°F). Stream sugar syrup into eggs while whipping on high. When ribbon stage is reached, fold into whipped cream. Fold in warm melted chocolate.

Transfer mousse to a serving bowl or to individual serving cups. Chill at least 2–3 hours before serving.

COWBELL

8801 Oak Street
(504) 298-8689
cowbell-nola.com

Chef Brack May began his New Orleans restaurant life at a cool place in the Central Business District called Cobalt. He was an innovator and the guy who introduced New Orleans diners to Chicken & Waffles, his way—crispy fried chicken with brown gravy and Steen's cane syrup, mashed potatoes on the side. His style tends toward eclectic modern, and he is always animated and a ton of fun. Cobalt closed, but Brack stayed around the city and lent his considerable skills to a number of restaurant/food-related projects both in and outside Louisiana. One day, on a visit to Liberty's Kitchen (a food-service-based social enterprise serving at-risk youths by providing life and job skills) for lunch, I spotted Brack in the kitchen, assisting/training in the cafe, and helping them develop a school lunch catering service. He also talked about a project for a restaurant on the river end of newly reinvigorated Oak Street. That project was/is Cowbell. On the upscale casual menu are a thick burger with fine toppings, fish tacos, hanger steak, adult grilled cheeses, and food that happens on a whim. The desserts are simple and satisfying. Cowbell is quirky, fun, and always busy. Brack and his wife Krista are also quirky and fun—and big community activists and supporters. Sometimes there is nothing so fine as going into Cowbell, ordering the organic chili and cheese fries and an ice-cold beer, then firing up Brack with the latest gossip. Best. Entertainment. Ever.

LOUISIANA BLUE CRAB TAMALES WITH CHARRED TOMATILLO SALSA & FRESH AVOCADOS PREPARED BY CHEF BRACK MAY

(MAKES 10-12 TAMALES)

20 or so corn husks, soaked overnight in warm water

Cabbage leaves, for lining steamer

For the charred salsa:

12 tomatillos

1 small Spanish onion

1 poblano pepper

2 jalapeño peppers

8 cloves garlic, halved

Chopped cilantro, to taste

Lime juice, to taste

Salt and pepper, to taste

1 orange, cut into segments

3 chipotle peppers, seeded, bloomed in hot water

For the crab filling:

1 ancho chili, bloomed in warm water

2 tablespoons cream

½ pound claw crabmeat, any type

½ pound jumbo lump crabmeat, more if you like

2 tablespoons butter

Juice of 1 lime

2 tablespoons chopped cilantro

Salt and pepper to taste

3 tablespoons gruyère

For the tamale dough:

1 cup seasoned stock (corn, chicken, or shrimp)

1½ cups dry masa

6 ounces butter, lard, or vegetable shortening, at room temperature

2 teaspoons baking powder

½ teaspoon salt

Kernels from 2 ears fresh shucked corn

2 tablespoons chopped cilantro

¼ cup grated cheese, preferably aged dry jack

For the avocado garnish:

3 large avocados, sliced

½ small red onion, chopped

¼ cup chopped cilantro

To make the charred salsa: Remove husks from tomatillos. Chop tomatillos and onion roughly, and place in a bowl. Remove seeds from poblano pepper and one of the jalapeños. In a broiler or on a grill, char the peppers until blistered but not totally incinerated. Leaving the charred skin on, puree the peppers and garlic then add to the bowl, along with cilantro, lime juice, salt, and pepper to taste. (This makes a great base for chunky salsa, too.) Fold in orange segments. Puree the chipotle peppers and stir them in. Cool and reserve.

To make the crab filling: Steep the ancho in the cream, and puree.

Sauté the crab gingerly in the butter. Add lime juice, cilantro, salt, and pepper. Loosen mixture with the ancho-cream puree, allow to cool, then fold in the cheese. Reseason and chill in the refrigerator until cold.

To make the tamale dough: Warm the stock and stir in the dry masa. (This equals 2 cups fresh masa). Leave to cool.

Whip the fat until white and fluffy. Add the baking powder, then the masa, and blend. Add the salt, corn, cilantro, and cheese and whip for three minutes.

To make the tamales: As you take each husk from the soaking water, clean it out as needed, wiping with a damp towel to rid it of the corn silk.

Place a tablespoon of masa mixture in the middle of the husk and flatten out with wet fingers. Place a good tablespoon of the crab filling in the middle of the masa and slowly roll and fold each side over till the filling is mostly covered with the masa mixture. Fold the husk over and completely cover the masa to protect it while steaming. If you need two husks, go ahead. Fold the bottom of the package back opposite from the seam.

Use cabbage leaves and a few husks to line the bottom of a steamer. With more cabbage leaves, make a mound in the center. Arrange the tamales folded side down, leaning at a 45-degree angle. Place the steamer in a tall pot, cover, and steam.

The tamales will get steamed for about 35 minutes and then need to rest for about 6–7 minutes before moving and/or eating. They can be cooked ahead and resteamed from cold without any ill effect.

To serve, rip the top of the husk off to expose the cooked tamale, drizzle with charred salsa, and top with avocado slices, red onion, and cilantro. Eat a couple before anyone sees that you have made them.

SWEET POTATO PECAN PIE
(MAKES 6 INDIVIDUAL PIES)

For the pie dough:

¾ pound (3 sticks) cold unsalted butter

3 cups flour

⅓ cup sugar

½ teaspoon kosher salt

⅓ cup ice water, or less

1 egg, lightly beaten, for sealing rims

2–4 tablespoons heavy cream, for brushing

For the sweet potato filling:

4–5 sweet potatoes

2 tablespoons butter

5 ounces white sugar, plus 1 tablespoon for caramelizing

1 ounce all-purpose flour

¼ teaspoon ground cinnamon

⅛ teaspoon ground ginger

3 eggs

1 ounce maple syrup

1½ cups heavy cream

For the pecan "frangipane":

8 ounces pecans

8 ounces sugar

4 ounces butter

2 ounces all-purpose flour

2 egg yolks and 1 white

½ pound shelled whole pecans, for garnish

To make the dough: Cut the butter into ¼-inch dice and place in the freezer for 6–8 minutes. Remove and combine in a bowl with flour, sugar, and salt. Rub the butter and dry ingredients with your fingers to separate the butter pieces. Place in a food processor and pulse about 6 times. Slowly add enough ice water for the dough to ball up. Place on a floured surface and get the dough to come together without overworking. Wrap in plastic wrap and allow to rest for 1 hour in the refrigerator. Cut into 6 portions and ball up. Roll out on a floured surface into 5- to 6-inch disks about ¼ inch thick. Refrigerate again until ready to assemble.

To make the filling: Preheat oven to 325°F. Peel one small sweet potato and dice it. Wash the rest, pierce their skins, and place in the oven on a foil-lined tray. Put 1 tablespoon butter in a small baking dish in the oven. When it melts, toss diced sweet potato with the butter and 1 tablespoon sugar, and return to oven. Roast the dice until caramelized, and the whole sweet potatoes until soft. Remove and cool. Reserve dice for garnish.

Scoop potato flesh from skins and measure out 14 ounces. Place in bowl of mixer with remaining sugar and other ingredients. Blend, but do not whip, until smooth.

To make the "frangipane": Crush the pecans with the sugar in a food processor. Cream the butter into the nuts and sugar. Add the flour. When everything else is creamed, mix in the eggs with quick pulses.

Remove dough disks from fridge. Place a tablespoon of frangipane on the bottom of each disk and spread thin. Put a generous ¼ cup of sweet potato filling in the middle of the pie, leaving a 1-inch rim. Egg-wash the rim and then fold over, a small section at a time, until you have a little pie. Top with another tablespoon of the frangipane, some cooked sweet potato pieces, and a couple of pecans. Brush the pastry rim with heavy cream. Refrigerate the pies for 20 minutes.

Bake at 375°–400°F for about 25 minutes, rotating once or twice. Cool for 10 minutes and eat warm, perhaps with some freshly whipped cream or vanilla ice cream.

FARMERS MARKETS

New Orleans farmers markets are more than a place to grab fresh local produce, they function as an event, a social gathering, a hub of information, and more. Most markets also offer music, cooking demonstrations, kids' activities, book signings, and prepared foods made from farmer-vendor produce.

Of course the original New Orleans farmers market was the French Market in the French Quarter, near the Old U.S. Mint. Historians tell us that the market site was a Native American trading place before New Orleans was New Orleans. It operated as a burgeoning public market, and by the end of the nineteenth century was a cultural collective where French, English, Spanish, German, Italian, Creole, and African languages could be heard. Early grocery entrepreneurs began with market stalls. The market flourished with butchers and fishmongers, cheese vendors and greengrocers from Saint Bernard Parish who trucked in produce to sell. That spawned roving street vendors and other spin-off markets that evolved citywide. In the 1930s and 1940s, public markets gave way to supermarkets and lost ground along with shoppers. By the mid-1990s the French Market had become a tourist destination for the flea market crammed with kitschy T-shirts, sunglasses, and knock-off designer watches.

However, across the country there was a resurgence of farmers markets, and New Orleans was not to be left out. In 1995 Richard McCarthy, executive director of Market Umbrella, and a dedicated group of like-minded folks launched the Crescent City Farmers Market with a mission to "cultivate the field of public markets, for public good." The first market opened that year in September, on Saturdays, and was an almost immediate success. From there came a Tuesday market uptown, a Wednesday market in Bywater, a Thursday late-afternoon market in Mid-City, and a Friday market out at the lakefront.

continued . . .

In addition, there are a slew of other public and seafood markets on the landscape. Today the list of farmers markets is bigger and better than ever. They exist beyond the Orleans Parish lines and make for a great day-trip.

THE FRENCH MARKET—Much more gussied up with covered areas and an indoor "kitchen stage" for cooking demonstrations, it is also the home of many food-related festivals. The produce is there along with locally made food products (hot sauces, jams, pickles, seasonings, and such). Crafts have replaced most of the junk.

CRESCENT CITY FARMERS MARKET (Uptown, Mid City, Bywater, Lakefront, downtown New Orleans)—The markets offer fresh produce, seafood, fish, meats, chicken, prepared foods, herbs, pastry, pesto, dairy, and native plants.

COVINGTON FARMERS MARKET (The Covington Trailhead, 419 N. New Hampshire)—For fresh produce, local goods, plants and prepared foods.

CAMELLIA CITY MARKET (The City Parking Lot at Robert Street and Front Street, Slidell)—Farmers market offering regionally grown fresh produce, "value added" goods and foods.

GRETNA FARMERS MARKET (Gretna Market Place, between 3rd and 4th Streets at 300 Huey P. Long Avenue, Gretna)—Rain-or-shine Gretna Farmers Market features more than thirty vendors offering a broad range of fruits and vegetables, meats and flowers.

VIETNAMESE FARMERS MARKET (14401 Alcee Fortier Boulevard, New Orleans East)—Twenty or more vendors set up blankets spread with produce, herbs, homemade tofu, eggs, and live chickens and ducks for sale. The courtyard houses shops selling Vietnamese baked goods and groceries.

WESTWEGO FARMERS AND FISHERIES MARKET (Sala Avenue at Fourth Street, Westwego)—More than fifty booths selling citrus, seafood, farm fresh eggs, jellies, pickles, fresh baked bread, cakes, pies, prepared foods, and crafts.

TUJAGUE'S

823 Decatur Street
(504) 525-8676
tujaguesrestaurant.com

Tujague's Restaurant has been holding down their Decatur Street corner for more than 160 years. New Orleans's second oldest restaurant is considered the place that gave birth to "second breakfast" or as we know it today, brunch. Cocktails are also an important element of Tujague's history, being the birthplace of both the Grasshopper and Whiskey Punch cocktails. As for the food, Tujague's is famously known for the Boiled Beef Brisket and Chicken Bonne Femme (pan sautéed chicken with a ham and potato hash). Owners Mark and Candace latter, together with Chef Thomas Robey, have created a restaurant experience that blends the traditional with the modern, tapping into local products and contemporary flavors and cooking technique. It's that mix of old and new that keeps Tujague's relevant, delicious and an inextricable part of New Orleans culinary fabric.

GRILLED YELLOWFIN TUNA
WITH CORN MAQUE CHOUX & SMOKED TOMATO BUTTER
(SERVES 4)

Four 8-ounce tuna steaks

4 tablespoons salad oil

Kosher salt and freshly ground black pepper

For the corn maque choux:

2 tablespoons vegetable oil

¼ cup chopped sweet onion

¼ cup chopped green bell pepper

1 garlic clove, minced

1½ cups fresh corn kernels

½ cup sliced fresh okra

½ cup peeled, seeded and diced tomato

¼ cup green onion, thinly sliced

Salt and freshly ground pepper to taste

For the smoked tomato butter

4 smoked or oven dried plum tomatoes, peeled

¼ cup melted butter

1 tablespoon cream

¼ teaspoon smoked paprika

1 splash cane vinegar

Salt and white pepper to taste

To prepare the corn maque choux: Heat vegetable oil in a large skillet over medium-high heat for 3 minutes. Add onion, bell pepper, and garlic and sauté for 5 minutes or until tender. Add corn, okra, and tomato; cook, stirring often, for 10 minutes. Add green onion and season with salt and pepper to taste.

To prepare the smoked tomato butter: Place all ingredients in a blender and mix well. Strain through fine-mesh strainer.

For the tuna: Get a charcoal or stovetop cast-iron grill very hot. Brush the fish with oil and sprinkle with salt and pepper. Grill each side for only 2–2 ½ minutes. The center should be rare, or the tuna will be tough and dry.

Allow tuna to rest for 5–10 minutes before serving.

CAVAN

3607 Magazine Street
(504) 509-7655
cavannola.com

Fresh on the heels of being crowned "King of Louisiana Seafood," Nathan Richard, a Louisiana native, is one of those chefs who leads by example. He's not only a talented cook with a big heart (consistently involved in charitable organizations and fundraisers), he teaches at Nicholl's State's John Folse Culinary School, and is a volunteer firefighter. Cavan, owned by entrepreneur Robert Leblanc's Leblanc & Smith Restaurant Group, is cool. A spunky, colorful dining space set inside a restored 19th century mansion, complete with distressed elements and low velvet seating. There are umbrella-covered outdoor dining tables nestled on the restaurant's front yard and porch. Weather permitting or in the relative cool of an evening, there's nothing so fine as sitting outside and digging in to Nathan's zucchini beignets and pecan-pest creme fraiche, or a satisfying bowl of gumbo with popcorn rice. Chef Nathan's homage to decadence is found in the Double (or triple) Stack Burger or his winning 2019 Seafood Cook Off dish Crawfish and Goat Cheese King Cake with Cream Cheese Pepper Jelly, Crab Fat, Sugar, and Cajun Caviar. A lovely brunch is served Friday–Sunday, featuring the dish Chef Nathan contributed here.

CAVAN SHRIMP & GRITS

(SERVES 4-6)

For the chili sauce base:

3 tablespoons garlic cloves, minced

3 tablespoons cup orange or satsuma zest

1 can chipotle peppers in adobo sauce

1 bunch cilantro, stems removed

For the chili sauce:

32 ounces orange juice or Satsuma juice

½ sprigs rosemary

½ shallot, minced

2–3 garlic cloves, smashed

1 bay leaf

1 ¼ pounds butter, cut into cubes

¼ cup chili sauce base (ingredients above and recipe below)

For the grits:

1 cup stone ground grits (You can use quick grits, if you must. Follow package directions subbing milk for water)

4 cups whole milk

¼ pound butter

1–2 tablespoons salt

To taste:

Seafood Magic® seasoning, to taste

Fresh ground black pepper, to taste

Crystal® hot sauce (or similar), to taste

For the shrimp:

1–2 pounds, 9–12 count shrimp, head on, tail on, shell removed, and deveined

3 tablespoons butter

To prepare the grits: Combine milk and butter in a large pot and bring to a slow simmer, while consistently whisking to be sure the milk and bottom of pot does not scald. After the butter is melted and milk is almost at a boiling point, whisk in the grits and salt. Reduce heat to very low and stir grits continuously for 5 minutes; afterwards stir every 5–7 minutes so mixture doesn't stick and burn. After roughly 1 hour, taste grits to check for doneness and proper seasoning. Place cooked grits on a large serving platter and keep warm.

To prepare the chili sauce base: Combine all ingredients in a food processor or blender until paste forms. This will yield approximately 1 cup

To prepare the chili butter sauce: Bring juice, rosemary, shallot, garlic, and bay leaf to a boil, and reduce by ⅓. Strain juice through a chinois to remove all aromatics. Place strained juice in a medium saucepot, and keep warm. Using an immersion blender (large stick blender) or blender slowly and carefully emulsify butter, several cubes at a time, into juice with blender is running. After all butter is incorporated add ⅓ cup of chili sauce base, and continue mixing for a minute.

To prepare the shrimp: In a cast-iron skillet over medium heat, add 3 tablespoons of butter, when the butter has completely melted add season shrimp, turning the shrimp only once. Add the chili butter sauce mixture to the pan and cook the shrimp for an additional 5 minutes. Remove shrimp from the pan, reserving sauce.

To serve: Place cooked shrimp atop of warm, plated grits. Spoon reserved butter sauce over the shrimp, and serve immediately. Use Seafood Magic®, Fresh Ground pepper or Crystal® hot sauce to your taste.

CAVAN KEY LIME PIE

(YIELDS: 1 PIE)

For the crust:

1 ¼ cups graham cracker crumbs

¼ cup sugar

1 teaspoon salt

1 stick of butter, melted

For the filling:

4 egg yolks

1 14-ounce can condensed milk

⅔ cups key lime juice

2 teaspoons grated zest and juice from 1 regular lime

To prepare the crust: Preheat oven to 325°F. Combine dry ingredients in a bowl. Slowly pour in melted butter and combine. Grease a springform pan and pour in the graham cracker mixture. Using a ½ cup measuring cup, smooth down the bottom and work the crust up the sides of the pan. The crust should come up to the top of the measuring cup. Continue to pack the crust until it is tight and firm around the sides. Place crust in the oven and cook for 10 minutes or until it is a light golden brown. Let cool before filling.

To prepare the filling: Place yolks in the bowl of a stand mixer fitted with the whip attachment. Whip until the yolks are pale, have increased in volume, and have a thick consistency. Slowly add the condensed milk and whip for another minute or until it is combined. Add the key lime juice along with the zest and regular lime juice, whip for another minute.

To make the pie: Preheat oven to 300°F. Pour filling into the pre-baked pie crust. Bake for 30–35 minutes. The center will still jiggle, but will be firm. If the center is still runny or not set, continue baking until it is set. Let the pie cool to room temp. Freeze overnight and let thaw in the fridge before serving.

MCCLURE'S BARBECUE

3001 Tchoupitoulas Street
(504) 301-2367
mccluresbarbecue.com

There's a lot to say about Chef Neil McClure. One of the most affable guys to grace the New Orleans restaurant industry, Neil has a vast history running several beloved and no-longer-with us restaurants: Figaro and, sigh, Dante's Kitchen (in the original version of this book). Neil is a barbecue fanatic in the way that all who are into barbecue are fanatical; that is to say he lives and breathes the craft. Long hours spent tending his pit smoker are only a fraction of his devotion to que. Everything from the meats, wood, sides, and sauces (he hand-makes six different varieties) are painstakingly selected and/or prepared. The greens (recipe below) are made with locally grown, hand picked, washed and massaged leaves. When Neil does fried chicken, get it and make sure to drag pieces through his stunning white Alabama-style sauce—it's the perfect combination of fat, salt, and acid. Chef Neil operates from the zero-waste mindset taking left-over meats and turning them into brilliant specials like Smoked Brisket Pho, a sort of Gyro, hand pies, and a million other creative things that fling from his busy, creative mind. The Jambalaya was born for such musings and left over bits of barbecue. It makes the best party food.

JAMBALAYA
(SERVES A CROWD)

¾ gallon stock

6 cups cooked rice

1 cup oil

1 cup green peppers smoked diced

1 cup onions smoked diced

½ pint mushrooms smoked diced

¼ cup garlic smoked fine diced

½ pint rub

⅓ cup kosher salt

3 tablespoons black pepper

1 tablespoon hot sauce

3 tablespoons your favorite barbecue sauce

1–2 bay leaves

½ cup brisket, chopped

1 cup pork, chopped

1 cup chicken, chopped

½ pound sausage, sliced

Heat oil in a large stock pot. Add all vegetables except mushrooms, and stir until heated and translucent. Add spices, hot sauce, and barbecue sauce. Stir thoroughly. Add meat and heat, stirring frequently

Add water to mixture and return to boil. Add rice. Stir. Return to boil. Put heat on low. Add mushrooms. Cook covered for 20 minutes, stirring occasionally to keep rice from sticking. Turn off heat when mixture is a saucy/sticky texture. Pour out onto a large sheet pan to cool.

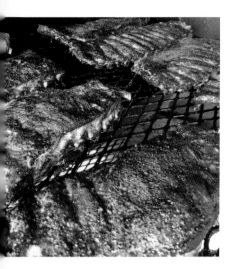

COLLARD GREENS

(SERVES A CROWD)

3 each, 2 pound cut & CLEANED greens

½ pound bacon

½ pound leftover rib meat

2 cloves smoked garlic (or use regular garlic and add a dash of liquid smoke to the pot)

2 smoked onions, dice

1–2 teaspoon your favorite barbecue rub

1¼ tablespoon salt

1¼ tablespoon black pepper

¾ cup molasses

¼ cup honey

1 cup hot sauce

2 cups apple cider vinegar

1½ cups brown sugar

2 cups water

Cook bacon until almost crisp. Add rib meat, garlic, onion and cook for a few minutes, stirring. Add spices and stir. Add hot sauce, honey, molasses, and vinegar, stirring well. Add water and bring to boil. Add sugar and stir until dissolved. Add greens, stir and cook over medium heat, slightly reducing liquid. Cover and cook until tender, stirring every 10 minutes.

YE OLDE COLLEGE INN

3000 South Carrollton Avenue
(504) 866-3683
collegeinn1933.com

Ye Olde College Inn is not only a restaurant, it's a happening, an event, a landmark. People of an age remember the days of carhop service, "parking," po-boys and familiar plates of hamburger steak, breaded veal cutlets, chicken-fried steak, red beans and rice, and pickled beet salad. The restaurant was opened in 1933 by the Rufin family and held by them until 2003, when the Blancher family bought College Inn. Two years into the Blanchers' restaurant ownership, and after restoring the damage done by Hurricane Katrina, they moved their popular bowling lanes and music venue, Rock 'n' Bowl, from Tulane Avenue to Carrollton, immediately abutting the "new" College Inn. A handful of the old items are still on the menu, right alongside a wider range of new dishes created by Johnny Blancher Jr. and the kitchen team. Much of the food includes ingredients plucked from the restaurant's nearby raised-bed gardens or local farmers markets. The Blanchers love to say, "College Inn and Rock 'n' Bowl is your one-stop place to dine and rock." As we say in New Orleans, "True dat."

SWEET POTATO—ANDOUILLE SOUP

(SERVES 10–12)

½ pound andouille sausage, diced

2 onions, diced

3 ounces Grand Marnier

3 sweet potatoes, peeled and diced

1 ounce honey

½ teaspoon cayenne pepper

1 teaspoon cinnamon

1 bay leaf

½ gallon whole milk

Salt and pepper to taste

Brown the diced sausage in a 3-gallon stockpot. Add diced onions and sweat until translucent. Add Grand Marnier and reduce until almost dry. Add sweet potatoes and 2 quarts water. Bring to a simmer and cook for 35 minutes or until potatoes are soft. Add honey, cayenne, cinnamon, and bay leaf. With an immersion blender, or working in batches with a food processor, blend soup mixture until smooth. Add milk, and season with salt and pepper. Serve hot.

ARNAUD'S

813 Bienville Street
(504) 523-5433
arnaudsrestaurant.com

Arnaud's holds a very special place in my heart. It was the very first restaurant I went to when I got here over 40 years ago. Alone, age 17, I walked in the door, marveled at the elegant and lively interior, and sat at a table where the waiter brought me Coquilles S. Jacques (it was still being made!). As I ate and enjoyed the food and the room, I saw a waiter preparing a flaming, tableside drink. Entranced, I watched as flambeed liquor licked down a curl of clove studded orange peel into a silver bowl, and then the contents were ladled into fancy glasses. The waiter noticed my interest, and a few minutes later, came to my table to present a slim ceramic cup filled with Cafe Brulot, a warm, liquor-laced coffee drink. It was spectacular. That was my first night in New Orleans, my first Cafe Brulot and my first "lagniappe" (a freebie). I'd found my home. The Casbarian

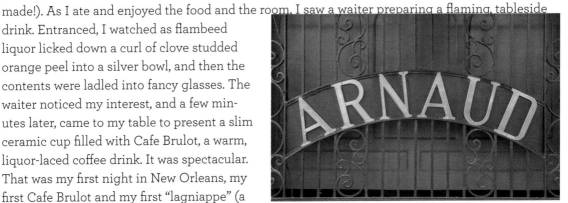

family (Miss Jane, Katy, and Archie), Chef Tommy DiGiovanni and the entire staff are beyond gracious and keepers of that all-important "grande dame" flame, as one of our over 100 year-old restaurants. The food is classic French Creole and it's fabulous. When it's on the menu, I'm particularly fond of Chef Tommy's sweetbreads preparation and though it'll likely get me in trouble, Shrimp Arnaud is without peer as the best shrimp remoulade in the city. After dinner, stroll into The French 75 bar for a cocktail or three.

TROUT AMANDINE
(SERVES 6)

1 cup (2 sticks) butter, unsalted

1 cup almonds, blanched and sliced

1 each lemon, juiced

1 teaspoon flat leaf parsley, finely chopped

Vegetable oil for deep frying

6 8-ounce, skinless, speckled trout fillets

1½ cups all-purpose flour

Kosher or sea salt, to taste

Freshly ground black pepper, to taste

Thinly sliced lemon slices and finely chopped flat-leaf parsley for garnish

Heat the oven to its lowest setting and place a baking sheet lined with a double layer of paper towels inside.

Place six dinner plates in the oven (on a lower rack) to warm.

In a small skillet, melt about ½ cup of the butter

over low heat. Add the almonds and stir and turn gently until they are uniformly golden, 5–7 minutes.

Remove the almonds from the pan with a slotted spoon, place in a bowl and set aside.

Add the remaining butter to the same skillet. When it is melted, stir in the lemon juice and parsley. Add salt and pepper to taste and taste for seasoning. Set aside while you fry the fish.

Place the flour in a large, shallow bowl near the stove and season generously with salt and pepper. In an electric deep fryer or a deep, heavy saucepan or stock pot no more than half filled with oil, heat the oil to 350°F.

Dredge two of the fillets in the seasoned flour, coating both sides. Shake off any excess flour and gently lower the fillets into the hot oil.

When the first two fillets are golden brown, remove with a skimmer basket and transfer to the towel-lined baking sheet to drain and keep warm while you fry the remaining fillets in the same way (Do not dredge the fillets until just before frying, or the coating will be gummy).

Return the lemon butter sauce to high heat and stir for a minute or two, until piping hot.

Place each fillet on a hot plate and scatter generously with the almonds.

Drizzle with some of the lemon-butter sauce

Garnish with the parsley and thinly sliced lemons and serve at once.

RALPH'S ON THE PARK

900 City Park Avenue
(504) 488-1000
ralphsonthepark.com

Ralph Brennan's namesake restaurant is gorgeous. Sharply appointed, painted in soothing colors, and encased by large plate glass windows that look upon the giant moss-hung oak trees and greenery of City Park. He's been in the business since he was a teenager, and as a part of an eponymous restaurant family, Ralph's on the Park is one of his eight "babies." Ralph describes this restaurant as "globally inspired local cuisine." At the kitchen helm is the equally passionate executive chef Chip Flanagan. Chip's food is serious, yet playful—Roof Bacon (rooftop-smoked bacon with fresh local pea shoots) is among his many creative creations. A passionate advocate for local and regional products, Chip is often spotted at local farmers markets, shopping, eating, and on occasion dishing up a Green Plate Special. He has a great sense of humor, is laid back, fun, and smart. One of his shining attributes is being comfortable with both local and ethnic cuisines, and his menu reflects sensible updates to New Orleans favorites with eclectic twists. "Brunch on the Park" is a perfect example of tweaked tradition—Turtle Soup followed by Braised Lamb (lamb ragout, cream cheese grits, fried egg, redeye gravy) and a finale of White Chocolate Bread Pudding that's become a New Orleans elevated classic.

MASA FRIED OYSTERS WITH CRISPY PORK BELLY & LEMON SAUCE
(SERVES 4 AS APPETIZER)

For the pork belly:

½ cup salt

½ cup sugar

1 slab pork belly, skinless (can use thick-cut bacon)

For the lemon sauce:

3 large lemons

1 cup cane sugar

6 ounces cane vinegar

Pinch of salt and pepper

For the masa fried oysters:

Cooking oil, as needed

1 cup masa flour

2 teaspoons salt

1 teaspoon ground black pepper

12 oysters

12 (1-ounce) slices slow-roasted pork belly

4 ounces lemon sauce

Sweet corn sprouts, for garnish

To make the pork belly: Combine salt and sugar and sprinkle all over the pork belly. Place curing belly in a plastic bag and refrigerate. Let belly cure overnight. The next day, preheat the oven to 250°F. Remove belly from bag and wipe off any cure that remains. Place belly in a roasting pan and cover with a lid or foil. Slow-roast the pork belly until the internal temperature reaches 165°F. This will take several hours; do not rush it. When temperature is reached, remove the belly from the oven and let cool

in the roasting pan. When it is cool enough to handle, place in the refrigerator for a few hours. When it is fully chilled, it can be easily sliced. Slice off a strip of belly and cut 1 ounce portions. Repeat until there are 12 rectangles.

Refrigerate the rest of the slab and use it with everything. For a treat, roast the belly on top of peeled carrots . . . delicious.

To make the lemon sauce: Remove the rind and white pith from the lemons. Place pulp and juice in a saucepot with the sugar, vinegar, and 1 cup water. Bring to a boil. Turn heat down to a simmer and cook for 30 minutes, or until a syrupy consistency is achieved. Strain out pulp and seeds and discard. Season the sauce with salt and pepper.

To make the fried oysters: In a heavy skillet, pour cooking oil to a depth of ½ inch. Set over medium-high heat. If using a thermometer, heat oil to 360° to 370°F.

Season the masa with the salt and pepper. Dredge the oysters in the seasoned masa. Drop a small pinch of masa in the oil. If it sizzles and bubbles, then the oil is ready. Carefully place the oysters in the oil, one at a time. Cook for about 90 seconds, turn the oysters over, and cook for 1 minute more. Remove the oysters from the oil and drain on layers of paper towels.

Place the slices of pork belly in the same oil and cook until browned and crisp, about 3 minutes. Remove the belly and drain with the oysters.

To serve, spoon lemon sauce onto four plates. Set 3 pork belly slices on each plate and set oysters on the belly pieces. Garnish with sweet corn sprouts.

STUFFED PEACH SNO-BALL
(SERVES 8)

For the peach granita:

2 cups ripe peaches, pitted

2 cups iced water

⅓ cup sugar

2 tablespoons lemon juice

Pinch of salt

For the sparkling sabayon cream:

7 egg yolks

⅓ cup sugar

1½ tablespoons honey

2 cups sparkling wine

½ cup cream

For the assembly:

8 ripe peaches

8 martini glasses

8 mint leaves, for garnish

To make the granita: Combine all ingredients in a blender until smooth. Pass through a fine mesh strainer. Adjust seasoning with lemon, salt, or sugar. Pour into a shallow pan and place in the freezer. Stir mixture with a fork every 30 minutes until frozen.

The granita can be made a day in advance. When ready to serve, remove from freezer and let sit for 10 minutes. Scrape with a fork into ice crystals.

To make the cream: First prepare an ice bath, and set a pot of water to boil. Choose a bowl or basin that will sit on the pot of water. In it combine the yolks, sugar, and honey and whisk until lighter in color. Add wine to yolk mixture. Place bowl over pot of boiling water. Whisk over heat until mixture becomes thick and airy. Chill mixture over ice bath, occasionally stirring gently.

In a chilled bowl, whip the cream to medium-peak consistency, and fold it into the chilled Sabayon.

This component should be prepared as close to serving time as possible, as it will begin to lose volume.

To assemble: Peel and dice the 8 peaches and distribute in the bottom of the martini glasses. Top the diced peaches with sabayon cream, but be sure to leave room for peach granita. Fill the glass with granita as high as possible, to resemble a New Orleans Sno-Ball. Garnish with a mint leaf and serve immediately.

TOUPS' MEATERY

845 North Carrollton Avenue
(504) 252-4999
toupsmeatery.com

With more than ten years in fine dining, Chef Isaac Toups craved to break out on his own and cook up sophisticated (but not too sophisticated) Louisiana dishes. Finally scoring a building that was once a Mediterranean restaurant on a busy stretch of Carrollton Avenue near City Park, Isaac and his wife Amanda renovated and opened this clean, blond-wood-bedecked restaurant bursting with creative and recognizable dishes from Isaac's hometown of Rayne, Louisiana. After only a few months, Toups' Meatery received high marks from local food writers for the house-cured charcuterie, crispy-fatty-fabulous cracklin's, pickles, massive cuts of meat, po-boys, and plates of stewy, slow-cooked foods. Isaac runs a tight, silent kitchen; his intensity is demonstrated in the plates of food that pour forth. Amanda is the "show girl," bubbling with personality at the front of house. The restaurant is consistently busy, with good reason. Amanda says, "We knew Isaac was good, that his food was good, though we didn't have a clue we'd be this popular this quickly. It's exciting!" Yes, it is.

CONFIT CHICKEN THIGHS, BUTTER BEANS, GREENS & GIZZARD GRAVY

(SERVES 4)

For the chicken:

4 chicken quarters, ribs removed

Kosher salt and black pepper

2 tablespoons fresh rosemary, finely chopped

2 tablespoons thyme

2 tablespoons oregano

10 cloves garlic

Duck fat as needed

Peanut oil as needed

For the beans:

1 tablespoon canola oil

1 onion, diced

2 ribs celery, diced

1 bell pepper, diced

6 strips smoked bacon, cut into 1-inch strips

2 bay leaves

1 pound dried butter beans

2–4 quarts chicken stock, as needed

Salt and cayenne pepper

2 tablespoons unsalted butter

For the greens:

1 tablespoon canola oil

2 cloves garlic, minced

Pinch of crushed red pepper flakes

1 bunch mustard greens

Pinch of salt

Juice of 1 lemon

For the gravy:

¼ cup flour

¼ cup canola oil

1 small onion, diced

2 cups chicken stock

6 ounces dark beer

1 pound chicken gizzards, cleaned and minced

1 teaspoon toasted ground cumin

1 tablespoon smoked paprika

Salt and pepper to taste

To make the confit of chicken: Season chicken generously with kosher salt and black pepper. Finely chop all herbs and garlic and mix well. Rub garlic and herb mixture into each side of thighs. Cover and refrigerate for 24 hours.

Place chicken in a baking dish or Dutch oven large enough to fit all thighs with 2 inches of clearance at the top. Completely cover chicken with equal parts rendered duck fat and peanut oil. Place in 225°F oven for two hours or until chicken is falling off the bone.

Remove with slotted spatula and place on plates. If not serving immediately, allow to cool, and reheat in fat.

To cook the beans: In a large Dutch oven, heat canola oil on medium heat. Sweat onion, celery, and bell pepper for 2 minutes, add bacon and cook for 1 minute more. Add bay leaves, beans, and enough chicken stock to cover by 3 inches. Bring mixture to a boil, taste water, and add salt and cayenne to taste. Lower to a simmer and let cook 2½–3 hours. Stir in butter right before serving.

To cook the greens: Heat canola oil on medium heat. Sauté garlic until golden brown, approximately 1 minute. Add pepper flakes, greens, and salt. Wilt for 1 minute until cooked through. Add lemon juice and serve.

To make the gravy: Cook flour and oil to make a light roux the color of café au lait. Sweat onions in the roux for 1 minute. Add chicken stock and beer, and bring to a boil. Add gizzards (Isaac grinds his gizzards in a meat grinder, but that may not be an option for most home cooks), cumin, paprika, and salt and pepper to taste. Lower fire to a simmer and cook for 2 hours.

BACCHANAL

600 Poland Avenue
(504) 948-9111
bacchanalwine.com

The weather-worn building that is Bacchanal began as a cool wine shop located at the far end of the Bywater neighborhood. There has since been an expansion, including a treehouse-like dining space to go with the wine "cave" and the backyard where lazy evenings, pop up dinners and chill parties happen with live local music. Hungry and thirsty folks hang in all three parts of the place. The Chef-Owner Joaquin Rodas continues to run the show from a more managerial position and there is a crack culinary team rolling out the eclectic bistro fare. Bacchanal also has its own culinary garden run by the brilliant and green-thumbed Chef Jo Larocca. It's stunning and her Instagram posts on @bacchanalgarden are glorious. Still, I harken back to the days when Chef Joaquin made ramen and his deep, dusky stew-soup pozole. Want something sweet to get that dance mojo working? The chocolate bark is salty-sweet goodness to fuel the fire.

BRAISED PORK SHOULDER POZOLE

(SERVES 4-6)

2 pounds pork shoulder, cut into fist-size cubes

Salt and pepper

4 tablespoons canola oil

10 cloves garlic, peeled

3 yellow onions, sliced

1 pint grape tomatoes

2 bottles Mexican beer

2 cups chicken stock

1 medium (28-ounce) can white hominy, drained and rinsed

2 sprigs cilantro

2 tablespoons Mexican oregano, plus more for garnish

½ head iceberg lettuce, thinly sliced

2 white onions, sliced, marinated in white vinegar for 1 hour

1 bunch cilantro, chopped

4 limes, quartered

Pat the pork pieces dry with paper towels. Sprinkle generously with salt and pepper. In a large overproof braising pan, heat canola oil, enough to coat the bottom, on medium-high heat. Working in batches, taking care not to crowd the pan or stir much, brown the meat on all sides. Once it has browned, transfer it to a bowl.

Preheat oven to 300°F.

Add garlic, onions, and grape tomatoes to pan. Stir well so as to not let anything burn. Once the onions and tomatoes start to release water, stir less frequently. Cook until onions are translucent, then add the beer. Reduce beer by half, add the chicken stock, and bring to a boil. Return the pork to the pan. Bring back to a boil, cover with a tight-fitting lid or aluminum foil, and place in the oven for 4 hours.

After 2 hours add the rinsed hominy, cilantro sprigs, 2 tablespoons oregano, and 1 tablespoon salt. Return to oven for remaining 2 hours, after which the pork should be fork tender and have a nice caramelized hue.

Divide the pozole on serving plates. Garnish with shaved iceberg lettuce, marinated onions, cilantro, and lime wedges. Finish with a shower of Mexican oregano rubbed between your hands.

DARK CHOCOLATE BARK

(MAKES 1¼ POUNDS OF BARK)

2 cups bittersweet chocolate (54% cocoa is ideal), chopped into small pieces

¾ cup roasted and peeled Marcona almonds

5 tablespoons extra virgin olive oil

2 tablespoons top-quality sea salt, such as Maldon or fleur de sel

Pinch of chili threads or cayenne pepper (optional)

Place a pot of water on the stove on medium-high heat. Once water starts to boil, place a metal mixing bowl on top of the pot. Choose a bowl that fits deeply in the pot, yet covers the rim so as to keep the steam from escaping. Put chopped chocolate in the bowl and melt it.

In a food processor, pulse the almonds until they are finely chopped, almost dust. Once chocolate is melted, fold in the almonds and incorporate completely.

Place parchment paper on a baking sheet, using adhesive tape to keep the paper at bay. Carefully remove the bowl of melted chocolate from the pot of boiling water and pour about half the chocolate onto the baking sheet. With a spatula, spread the chocolate until it is very thin. (Put some back into the bowl if necessary.) Set the baking sheet in the refrigerator, level, until chocolate hardens completely. Repeat with remaining chocolate.

To plate, break chocolate into jagged shards, place on plates, drizzle with extra virgin olive oil, and strew with salt and, if you like, chili threads.

CAKE CAFÉ & BAKERY

2440 Chartres Street
(504) 943-0010
nolacakes.com

This corner bakery cum cafe evokes the feeling of being in a beloved aunt's kitchen, where warm yeast scents are heavy on the air, coffee is brewing, and cupcakes tempt from the pastry case. Chef Steve Himelfarb started his culinary tenure as "the cake man" selling fat individual cake slices to patrons and businesses along Magazine Street. Roll forward a number of years, and a short time at a teeny space on Exchange Alley in the French Quarter, to his current Marigny digs. Here, along with the pastries there are giant, fluffy biscuits piled with eggs and ham, omelets, grits, tofu scramble, fried oyster sandwiches (when oysters are in season), meatloaf, salads, and all manners of soul-satisfying soups. One of Steve's famous cupcakes can be added to any meat for a dollar; the difficulty is in choosing from among the daily flavors that can include double chocolate, wedding cake, mimosa, red velvet, or even Sazerac. Always innovating, Chef Steve and his bakery team came up with Mardi Gras's wildly popular, bold purple-green-and-gold-icing-striped King Cakes filled with goat cheese and apples. Year round, spot hilariously decadent items in the case like the walnut-filled Buddha Hands, the Deep-Fried Chocolate Croissant, or the genius Quichant that can be a carnivore or herbivore's dream. Steve shared the Quichant because "They are seriously delicious and probably the most fun thing someone would want to make at home."

QUICHANT

Making homemade croissant and puff pastry is a labor of love, and a labor. If you're committed to the process, that's incredible, but for this recipe Chef Steve says that store-bought dough and puff pastry tart shells are perfectly wonderful.

(SERVES 10-12)

10–12 best-quality frozen puff pastry tart shells

10–12 best-quality store-bought croissant or fine crescent-roll dough

12 eggs

½ cup half-and-half

Optional filling ingredients:

Bacon, cooked and crumbled

Cheddar cheese, grated

Red or yellow onion, diced

Roasted red peppers

Fresh goat cheese, crumbled

Fold croissant/crescent roll dough to fit into the bottom of the tart shell. Place on parchment lined cookie sheet. Chill for 30 minutes.

While the dough-lined tart shells are chilling, gather your filling ingredients—perhaps bacon, cheddar, and onion for the carnivores or roasted red peppers, goat cheese, and onion for vegetarians—about 2 tablespoons altogether per tart. Put fillings into shells and chill again for 15 minutes.

Whip the eggs together with the half-and-half. Pour mixture into the shells, over fillings, almost to the top of the shell. Bake quichants at 350°F for 20–25 minutes, until top is golden and filling is firm but slightly wobbly. Cool and serve warm or at room temperature.

ELIZABETH'S

601 Gallier Street
(504) 944-9272
elizabethsrestaurantnola.com

If there is one thing people know about Elizabeth's, it's the praline bacon. To be sure, it's very, very good, but Chef Bryon Peck is about more than praline bacon, even if that was what put Elizabeth's on the map. Adhering to the original owner's philosophy of "Real food, done real good," Bryon has long cooked or cooked-and-managed at Elizabeth's, and it finally and officially became his in 2011. The hundred-year-old building functioned as a catering kitchen in 1996, then a restaurant, went through a succession of owners, and now, fully in Bryon's hands, has really hit its culinary stride. The menu is broad-ranging at breakfast, lunch, dinner, and brunch, with everything from burgers to seafood, French toast, and cocktails. The fried chicken livers with homemade pepper jelly are astounding, and there is crazy love for the strawberry-stuffed French toast, the Dream Burger with praline bacon and blue cheese (ooh, that sweet-tangy-salty thing), and fork-tender pork osso bucco over a fried grit cake. The huge menu also boasts crab cakes, frog legs, scallops, fish, meat, and at brunch a Duck Waffle (sweet potato and duck hash atop a cornbread waffle) or these hunger-inducing dishes for which Bryon has generously provided his recipes.

BAKED OYSTERS WITH FOIE GRAS & TRUFFLE AIOLI

Combining briny local bivalves and the richness of foie gras (happily not banned in New Orleans) with a wee drizzle of truffle oil, this is nothing but utter decadence.

(SERVES 6–8)

10 ounces foie gras

4 egg yolks

1 tablespoon Dijon mustard

Juice of 1 lemon

2 ounces good-quality truffle oil

Salt

24 P&J oysters in the shell

Start by rendering the foie over slow heat in a thick-bottomed pot, not allowing it to color. This will take at least 30 minutes. Remove foie from heat when fully rendered. Let set and cool until it reaches 120°F.

Start making aioli, in a Cuisinart or in a bowl with a stick blender, by blending the yolks with the mustard and lemon juice. Now slowly add truffle oil, then foie gras fat. As it thickens, thin with water. At the end add all rendered foie gras and its fat; again remember to thin out with water—perhaps 2 ounces in all. Finish by adding salt to taste.

Open oysters and loosen them from their shells, keeping each in its bottom shell-half. Top with aioli and put under broiler until sauce is golden and oysters are warm.

SALMON & BRIE GRILLED CHEESE TOPPED WITH FRIED EGGS

(SERVES 4)

For the grilled cheese:

8 slices seeded rye bread

8 ounces brie cheese

6 ounces smoked Nova salmon, approximately 4 slices

Butter as needed

For the eggs:

Butter for frying

8 fresh eggs

Curly parsley, chopped, for garnish

Red onion, minced, for garnish

To make the sandwiches: Remove crusts from the bread and cut each slice into two rectangles. Lay bread on a cutting board. Cut brie into sixteen equal pieces and place on bread rectangles. Cut salmon into eight equal pieces and place them on half of the brie-topped bread slices. Fold over the other eight halves of brie-topped bread onto them to make sandwiches. Butter both sides of sandwiches generously, and grill.

To cook the eggs: In a nonstick skillet, melt butter. Fry eggs over easy. Place on top of grilled cheese sandwiches and garnish with chopped parsley and onion.

JACK ROSE

2031 St. Charles Avenue
(504) 323-1500
jackroserestaurant.com

Inside the Pontchartrain Hotel on St. Charles Avenue is a warren of dining rooms all raucously decorated. Jack Rose is colorful and comfortable, the handiwork of Chef Brian Landry and business partner Emery Whalen, principles of QED Hospitality group. Their Chef de Cuisine, whip smart David Whitmore, together with his kitchen crew have created a fun menu of innovative dishes like Fried Chicken Parmesan and Crawfish Bread with heady, gooey Raclette cheese. Snazzy cocktails partner the modern, approachable food. There is a killer Friday with all-you-can-drink bubbles, and any number of people drinking from a "Chambong." It's hilarious. Sunday brunch features Quail & Waffles with cane syrup, duck confit hash and a really good burger to cure what ails. Save room for dessert, because there's Mile High Pie with chocolate sauce; and a peanut butter and marshmallow ice cream Fluffernutter Sundae studded with caramel blondie bites. Chef David and Brian shared one of the restaurant dishes that appears on each and every menu, except dessert. It's an homage to our Mighty Mississippi River and sweet Louisiana shrimp.

SHRIMP "MUDDY WATERS"
(SERVES 4)

2 tablespoons extra virgin olive oil

½ cup onion, minced

½ cup celery, minced

½ cup carrot, minced

¼ cup garlic, minced

½ teaspoon red chili flakes

1 tablespoon tomato paste

1 cup dry white wine

½ tablespoon kosher salt

½ tablespoon sugar

1 tablespoon oregano, chopped

1 quart strong shrimp stock

5 pounds, 10–15 count Royal Red Shrimp

3 tablespoons kosher salt

1 tablespoon black pepper

3 tablespoons olive oil

4 tablespoons butter, cubed

Peel and devein the shrimp. Season with salt and pepper and place in refrigerator. Place the shrimp shells in 1.5 quart saucepan, cover with water, and bring to a simmer. Allow shells to simmer for 30–45 minutes. Strain the stock from the shells.

In a separate 2-quart sauce pan sweat the onion, celery, and carrot for 4–5 minutes or until aromatic. Add garlic, chili flakes, and tomato paste and sweat for 2–3 more minutes. Deglaze with the white wine. Add salt, sugar, and oregano. Allow contents to come to a boil and reduce by half.

Add shrimp stock and simmer for 15 minutes or until all flavors have had a chance to mesh.

Heat olive oil in a cast iron skillet over medium-high heat. In small batches sear the shrimp on both sides until golden brown and just cooked through (be careful not to overcook). Return all of the shrimp to the cast iron skillet and pour the muddy waters sauce over the top. Add the butter a few cubes at a time and stir until well incorporated. Sauce should be a rich brown color with a "muddy" hue.

Shrimp muddy waters can be served with grits, over your favorite pasta, or with rice. At Jack Rose we serve it with squid ink campanelle pasta.

SATSUMA CAFE

3218 Dauphine Street, (504) 304-5962
7901 Maple Street, (504) 309-5557
1320 Magazine Street (504) 354-9869
satsumacafe.com

In 2009 when Cassi and Peter Dymond opened Satsuma Cafe in the former Coffea space, they kept the vibe pretty much as it was, with simple breakfast items, sandwiches, and so on. They did evolve the menu some, adding fresh juices and farmers market produce, eventually hiring white tablecloth-pedigreed chef Michael Costantini to take the food up a notch. These days, to call Satsuma Cafe a coffee shop is to give it short shrift. Though the menu is composed of breakfasts, salads, sandwiches, and fresh-pressed juices of locally sourced produce, there is a gourmet quality to the offerings that elevates the cafe's status—evidence the inclusion of chanterelles in egg dishes or lump crabmeat that dolls up a grilled cheese. The funky-eclectic interior remains the same, with mismatched tables, wild art, and all manner of reading materials strewn about, giving Satsuma its hippie chic feel. For a time, the gang added dinner service that drew solid notices, but sadly it didn't stick, and so they dropped the evening menu of stylish dishes, had Michael refine the menu, and began searching for a second location to do more and bigger at breakfast and lunch. In August 2012, Satsuma's Uptown location opened with Chef Michael's gentle menu refinements. The possibility of doing dinner looms, but for now there are simple, lovely dishes that even have fans like food-obsessed Michael Stipe of R.E.M. who wrote this: "Their Kale Salad, made of all local ingredients, fresh, and organic, features Lacinato kale, Parmesan dressing, and (this is New Orleans after all) a piece of bacon on the side. This is the BEST SALAD in the city, hands down." The newest location in a fancy build-out on lower Magazine Street, has a grassy knoll with tables and a seriously chill vibe. The coffee and food are rockin'.

WARM WINTER SALAD OF ROASTED, PICKLED & RAW VEGETABLES
(SERVES 6–8)

For the lemon vinaigrette:

¼ cup lemon juice

Zest of 2 lemons

1 teaspoon Dijon mustard

1 clove of garlic, microplaned

1 teaspoon chopped thyme

Pinch of salt

¼ cup canola oil

¼ cup extra virgin olive oil

For the pickled beet and red onion:

1 cup red wine vinegar

1 cup sugar

1 red beet, sliced

1 red onion, sliced thin

For the capers:

2 tablespoons capers, rinsed and dried

¼–½ cup canola oil

For the salad:

10 brussels sprouts

1 bunch Tuscan kale

¼ cup pickled red onion

½ butternut squash, top half only, peeled

2 carrots, peeled

2 parsnips, peeled

1 teaspoon salt

1 teaspoon pepper

1 tablespoon olive oil

4 (1½-inch) florets cauliflower

4 (1½-inch) florets broccoli

Freshly grated Parmigiano-Reggiano

Note: Make the lemon vinaigrette and pickled beet and red onion ahead. You can also make the capers ahead or right before serving, chef's choice.

To make the lemon vinaigrette: Mix the lemon juice and zest, mustard, garlic, thyme, and salt in a bowl with a whisk. Drip by drip add in the oils while whisking until an emulsion starts to form. Increase the stream and continue to whisk until oil is all incorporated.

To pickle the red onions: Put the vinegar, sugar, beet, and 1 cup water in a pot and bring to a boil. Pour over sliced onion and cover immediately. Let sit at room temperature for at least 8 hours, then refrigerate.

To fry the capers: Place the capers in a small pot and cover with canola oil. Turn up the heat and fry the capers until they are crispy. Strain the capers and place on a paper towel to dry. Reserve oil for another use, such as caper vinaigrette.

To make the warm winter salad: Using a benriner or mandoline, shred 5 brussels sprouts. Place in a large mixing bowl.

Remove thick ribs from the kale leaves, wash in cold water, dry, and slice into thin ribbons. Add to shredded brussels sprouts.

Add pickled red onions to bowl.

Using the mandoline, slice the squash and carrots into long ribbons about 1/8 inch thick and 1 inch wide. Using the same thickness setting, cut round slices out of the parsnips. Toss with half the salt, half the pepper, and half the olive oil.

Cut the other 5 brussels sprouts into quarters. Toss the cauliflower, broccoli, and quartered brussels sprouts with remaining salt, pepper, and olive oil, and lay on a sheet tray. Roast under the broiler until starting to get some dark coloring, almost burning, at which point add the squash, carrots, and parsnips. When the root vegetables start to soften, after a couple of minutes, remove from the heat and toss with the shredded brussels sprouts and kale and onions. Add some of the dressing, and taste for seasoning.

To serve: Arrange the salad in a heaping stack and cover with freshly grated Parmesan and a sprinkling of the crunchy fried capers.

SEASONAL FRUIT & ROSEMARY COBBLER
(SERVES 6)

5 cups of seasonal fruit—strawberries, blueberries, peaches, or plums

1½ cups sugar

2 tablespoons cornstarch or tapioca starch

Zest and juice of 1 lemon

1 teaspoon vanilla

2 tablespoons heavy cream

¼ cup turbinado sugar or coarse sugar, for sprinkling

For the dough:

3 cups all-purpose flour

4 teaspoons baking powder

1 tablespoon sugar

1 teaspoon salt

1 tablespoon finely chopped fresh rosemary

12 ounces (3 sticks) cold unsalted butter

1½ cups heavy cream, well chilled

For the vanilla whipped cream:

1 cup heavy whipping cream, well chilled

2 tablespoons powdered sugar

Seeds scraped from ½ vanilla bean, or 1 teaspoon
   vanilla extract

First make the dough. In a small bowl, sift together
the flour, baking powder, sugar, salt, and rosemary.
Cut the butter into the flour, using a pastry cutter or
two knives, until the butter is the size of small peas.
Add 1½ cups chilled cream gradually, mixing with a
wooden spoon or spatula, until a dough ball forms.

Refrigerate the dough until ready to use.

Butter six 6-ounce ramekins or one large baking
dish. If you are using stone fruits such as peaches
or plums, peel and slice them about ¼ inch thick.
If you are using strawberries, slice them in half. In
a large bowl, mix the fruit with the sugar, starch,
lemon zest and juice, and vanilla. Place the fruit
mixture in the ramekins or baking dish.

Preheat oven to 350°F. Drop the dough on top of the
fruit, making sure to spread it out so that it covers
the fruit. With a pastry brush, brush the top of the
dough with the heavy cream, and sprinkle with
turbinado sugar. Place the ramekins or baking dish
on a sheet tray. Bake for 30–35 minutes until the
cobbler is golden brown. Let cool.

When ready to serve, prepare the whipped cream
topping. In a cold bowl, whisk the cream, powdered
sugar, and vanilla seeds or extract just until peaks
form. Serve the cobbler warm with a dollop of the
fresh whipped cream.

THREE MUSES

536 Frenchmen Street
(504) 252-4801
thethreemuses.com

Marigny hip with retro flair: that describes what is Three Muses, opened in 2010 by Chef Daniel Esses and jazz singer Sophie Lee. Perfectly placed on hipper-than-hip Frenchmen Street, one of the city's musical hearts, Three Muses is a restaurant with great music and a club with great food and cocktails—it hits on all three cylinders. The restaurant-club interior is dark wood paneled, and the giant bar beckons patrons to kick off an evening with the house cocktail, the Muse: cucumbers, strawberries, St. Germain liqueur, and gin. Chef Daniel Esses's considerable background in white-tablecloth dining means food with a twist and an upscale sensibility. He is a craftsman and appreciates how to incorporate the flavors of Louisiana with ethnic, often Asian inspiration. His handmade pastas are often featured on the menu—he was once a vendor at the Tuesday Crescent City Farmers Market, selling those hand-rolled pastas and his sauces—as part of the vegetarian offerings. There is a lot to love on Dan's imaginative menu, from Steak & Cake (a quirky surf-and-turf that includes a crab cake), to crispy french fries tumbled with tangy feta and citrus-flecked gremolata, and even the sometimes special of an eggroll larded with lobster. Everything at Three Muses is vivid, energetic, and busy. A wait for a table is fairly common, but no big thing. The Three Muses rule is to relax, have a drink, a table will open soon. It's fine advice, allowing for time to be inspired by the Three Muses—music, food, and cocktails.

CIDER BRAISED PORK BELLY OVER SCALLION PANCAKE

(SERVES 4 –6)

For the pork belly:

1 cup hard cider

½ cup chicken stock

½ cup light soy sauce

2 tablespoons oyster sauce

2 pounds pork belly, in a slab

2 tablespoons Louisiana honey

2 tablespoons vegetable oil

For the apple chutney:

4 tablespoons vegetable oil

1 small onion, minced

2 cooking apples, peeled and minced

1 piece star anise

3 coriander seeds

1 allspice berry

2 tablespoons sugar

2 tablespoons apple vinegar or apple cider vinegar

1 crisp eating apple, julienned, for garnish

For the scallion pancakes:

1 tablespoon vegetable oil

2½ cups flour

Pinch of salt

2 tablespoons toasted sesame oil

1 cup minced scallions, green part only

Vegetable oil for frying

To make the pork belly: Preheat oven to 325°F.

Mix cider, chicken stock, soy sauce, and oyster sauce in a bowl.

Place pork belly in a roasting pan. Pour sauce over pork belly. Cover with foil. Cook pork until knife goes through easily, about 1½ hours. Cool. Strain juices and reserve.

Remove pork to a sheet tray and cover with parchment paper. Place another sheet tray of the same size over the pork and weight with a brick or other heavy object. Allow to set overnight.

Meanwhile, combine reserved cooking liquid with honey and mix well.

Take cooled pork belly and slice it into three rectangular pieces. Cut each rectangular piece crosswise into 1-inch slices.

Heat a nonstick sauté pan with a little vegetable oil. Add a few pieces of belly at a time. Cook on each side until golden brown, then remove and reserve. Once all the pieces you want have been cooked crisp, add cooking liquid to pan and reduce by half. Set aside until serving time.

To make the chutney: Heat oil in a large pan set over medium-high heat. Add onion and cook until translucent, about 5 minutes. Add apple and cook until it begin to soften, again about 5 minutes. Stir in star anise, coriander, allspice, and sugar. Cook for 5 minutes until blended. Add vinegar. Cook until apples are soft, about 5 minutes more.

To make the pancakes: Place vegetable oil and 1 cup water in a small pot over high heat and bring to a boil. Cool for 5 minutes.

Mix flour and salt in a large bowl. Pour water and oil mixture over flour. Mix with a wooden spoon, then use your hands to mix well. Cover with plastic wrap and allow to cool.

Divide dough into six even pieces and flatten into 4-inch disks. Mix sesame oil, salt, and scallions. Roll the coated disks in the mixture, then form them into balls. Flatten each ball again into a disk.

To assemble: Heat vegetable oil in a pan set over medium-high heat until a drop of water sizzles in the oil, about 2 minutes. Fry the pancakes in batches until crispy. Drain on paper towels. Place a scallion pancake on each serving plate.

Meanwhile, reheat the reduced pork belly liquid, add back the pork belly, and just coat each piece. Place on scallion pancakes, top with apple chutney, and garnish with crisp apple juliennes.

BANANA MASCARPONE STRUDEL

(SERVES 8)

For the banana caramel sauce:

1 cup sugar

1 cup heavy cream

2 tablespoons Myers's rum

1 banana, diced

For the mascarpone strudel:

1 pound mascarpone

½ cup cream

1 cup sugar

2 bananas, diced

1 cup chocolate chips

½ cup crushed pistachios

6 ounces unsalted butter, divided

6 sheets phyllo dough

To make the sauce: In a saucepan over medium heat, cook sugar with 1 cup water until it turns to a medium-dark caramel. Add cream and whisk until totally incorporated. When you put the cream in, it will not look right, but leave it on medium heat and whisk and it will blend together. Add rum and stir. Let cook for 5 minutes, then add the banana and cook for 5 more minutes. Let cool.

To make the strudel: In the bowl of a stand mixer fitted with the whisk attachment, combine mascarpone, cream, and sugar. Whisk on medium until incorporated, just a few minutes. (You can do this by hand, but make sure to mix well.) On low speed now, add bananas, chocolate chips, and pistachios. Just mix to incorporate. Let cool in the refrigerator for 30 minutes.

Melt ½ cup (1 stick) butter. Take one sheet of phyllo and brush with melted butter, then put another sheet on top, brush it with butter, and do the same with a third sheet. Place a few spoonfuls of mascarpone banana mixture along the bottom of the phyllo. Roll into a long log, and cut log into four even pieces. Repeat the process with the remaining three sheets of phyllo. Place strudel pieces in freezer for 1 hour.

In a large nonstick pan, melt 2 tablespoons butter until it sizzles, add 4 pieces of strudel, and brown for about 30 seconds on each side. Repeat.

Serve with banana caramel sauce and your favorite ice cream. At our restaurant we use Mexican Chocolate.

GW FINS

808 Bienville Street
(504) 581-3467
gwfins.com

Chef-owner Tenney Flynn is a fish guru. He's the go-to guy when a weary food writer wants to know what's really happening in the industry. GW Fins is the brainchild of Chef Tenney and his business partner Gary Wollerman (GW), the restaurant's wine sage. Both have strong restaurant chops, and at Fins there are no dangling details. The broad, open room is classically appointed, contemporary but comfy. The bar area is small but mighty, with solid bar keeps putting out great cocktails with or without frills. Gary is in charge of the stunning, enormous, and award-winning wine list. The food at Fins is seafood-centric with a southern charm and sensibility. Chef Tenney credits the roots of his cooking style and acumen to his Georgia upbringing and soul food cook/ teachers as well as his formal training. He has put Chef Mike Nelson in place as Executive Chef and the restaurant is at the top of its game. While Fins is a fine-dining seafood restaurant, the biscuits that are everyone's first bite draw sighs of joy. Don't ask what makes them extra fabulous: it's lard. GW Fins sources seafood globally and locally, pulling from the world's waters so that diners can experience Alaskan king crab, bay scallops from the Northeast, snapper from the Gulf, bass from New Zealand, and even Louisiana stone crab claws. All the seafood is prepared simply and unmasked—no heavy sauces cover the works. Global exploration is also tasted in the style and manner of preparation, as in the Asian-inflected recipe shared here. Chefs Tenney and Mike are seriously elective about the seafood that comes in the door of the restaurant, printing a new menu every day to showcase the latest catch. It's not all fine-dine and fancy this crew loves to be on-the-ground local participating in events in and out of the French Quarter, and their Fried Maine Lobster Po-Boy has taken first prize at the Oak Street Po-Boy Festival.

GW FINS SAUTÉED LOUISIANA RED SNAPPER WITH MUSSELS & THAI CURRY BROTH

(SERVES 4)

For the curry broth for mussels:

10 head-on U-15 shrimp

1 tablespoon olive oil

1 teaspoon diced ginger

1 shallot, diced

1 clove garlic, diced

1 kaffir lime leaf

3 basil stems, diced

2 tablespoons diced cilantro stems

1 lemongrass stalk, crushed and chopped

2 teaspoons green curry paste

2 cups shrimp stock

2 cans coconut milk

For the snapper with mussels:

2 pounds Maine or Prince Edward Island mussels

4 red snapper fillets, 7–8 ounces each, skin on

Salt and black pepper

Flour for dredging

2 tablespoons plus 1 teaspoon olive oil

2 tablespoons butter

¼ cup sliced chanterelles (optional)

1 link Chinese sausage, sliced thinly on the bias

Dash of fish sauce

5 cups curry broth for mussels

1 package fresh rice stick noodles

2 tablespoons chopped cilantro

2 tablespoons chopped Thai basil

To make the curry broth for mussels: Roughly chop the shrimp and sauté them in a little olive oil. Add the diced ginger, shallot, garlic, lime leaf, basil and cilantro stems, and lemongrass. Sweat-sauté for a few minutes on medium heat. Add the curry paste, and stir in the stock and 4 cups water. Cook at a low boil for 30 minutes. Add the coconut milk and return to a boil. Puree with an immersion blender and strain. Cool and refrigerate.

To cook the fish and soup: First, check mussels carefully to make sure they're alive. If open, gently squeeze the shells shut; if they're dead, the shell won't stay closed. Discard the dead ones.

Place four large pasta bowls in a warming oven.

Preheat a large, heavy sauté pans. Season the fillets on both sides with salt and pepper and dredge them in flour. Place 1 tablespoon olive oil and 1 tablespoon butter in each pan and place the fish in, two to a pan, skin side down. Cook 3–4 minutes and turn over.

Place 1 teaspoon olive oil in 4-quart pot and add the chanterelles and sliced sausage. Cook on medium

heat stirring often for 2 minutes. Add the mussels and raise the heat. Cover and cook for 1 minute more. Add a dash or two of fish sauce.

Add the 5 cups curry broth and bring to a boil. Break the rice noodles into 4-inch pieces and add half the package to the boiling broth. Cook for 10 seconds, stirring so the noodles are immersed in the boiling stock. Add half the chopped herbs, and ladle the soup into the preheated pasta bowls.

Place a snapper fillet, skin side up, in the center of each bowl and garnish with additional Thai basil and cilantro.

PIECE OF MEAT

3301 Bienville Street
(504) 372-2289
pieceofmeatbutcher.com

Piece of Meat was named among 2019's *Food & Wine* magazine Top 10 Best New Restaurants in the U.S. Located in Mid City, just off the snazzy new Lafitte Greenway bike-path that stretches from the French Quarter to right near City Park, this small but mighty butcher shop and restaurant rocks. Owner Chefs Leighann Smith and The Rev. Dr. Dan Jackson have worked together for a long time and their restaurant brings together their mutual love for butchery, food, cocktails and friends . . . and not necessarily in that order. The opening menu included a sleeper appetizer that went viral. Thousands of boudin egg rolls later, Chefs Leighann and Dan credit much to that app and of course the house-made bologna made famous at their pal's restaurant, Turkey and the Wolf. The smoker is always going and so are Dan and Leighann. On the menu is a nice selection of meats, sandwiches and sides; the cold case is packed with sausages, smoked duck legs, cured, smoked and aged meats, hot dogs, brisket, etc. There's always a special or two on the chalkboard, and in a small cooler near the cash-register find local eggs, butter, tubs of lard, cheese, smoked chicken salad and jars of silky chicken liver pate. There's weekend brunch, steak nights on the odd Tuesday, and about that butchering . . . Top quality beef, pork and chicken are local or regionally sourced, hand cut from primals and pretty dang close to perfect. When you get good at rolling these boudin egg rolls and are in New Orleans, come see Leighann, she's got a place for you in the kitchen.

BOUDIN EGG ROLLS

(YIELD: 4 EGG ROLLS)

For the sriracha mayo

1 cup mayo of your choice (I like Duke's)

¼ cup sriracha sauce

For the egg rolls:

2 links of boudin sausage from Piece of Meat (or your favorite brand)

2 ounces stick pepper jack cheese

Store-bought wonton wrappers

1 large egg, beaten

Vegetable oil, for frying

To make the sriracha mayo: Mix the mayo and sriracha in a small bowl until combined.

For the boudin egg rolls: Remove the boudin from the casing, separate each link in half and cut the pepper jack cheese into 2-by-½-inch sticks.

Make a patty out of each half link of boudin. Place a stick of cheese on the patty and roll it around the cheese to form a cigar-like shape. Place on a corner of a wonton wrapper. Roll and fold the wrapper like you would any egg roll, using the beaten egg to seal it. Repeat with the remaining boudin, cheese and wrappers.

In a large heavy-bottomed saucepan, pour enough oil to fill the pan about a third of the way. Heat over medium heat until a deep-frying thermometer inserted in the oil reaches 335°F. Fry the egg rolls in batches until golden, 5–8 minutes per batch. Let cool and enjoy!

RESTAURANT R'EVOLUTION

777 Bienville Street
(504) 553-2277
revolutionnola.com

Chefs John Folse and Rick Tramonto are a little bit country, and a little bit rock 'n' roll. It's an intriguing partnership that had been in the making for a couple of years before the doors to R'evolution finally swung open. After a lot of pomp and circumstance, dollars spent and the build-out completed, the Royal Sonesta Hotel now boasts a jaw-dropping multiroom restaurant evocative of a fine Creole mansion, complete with culinary ephemera, historic knickknacks, and a tricked-out kitchen that's the envy of every chef. Executing the gargantuan menu, Chef Jana Billiot brings her enormous talent to turning out a wild bouquet of styles, flavors, and foods from old Louisiana and the "seven nations" that are her composition—Italian, French, Spanish, German, Acadian, and Native and African American. The restaurant serves breakfast, brunch, lunch, and dinner of interpreted classics like gumbo and jambalaya, or corn and crab soup, as well as a host of meats, charcuterie, pastas, and specialty items like the Triptych of Pork (pork belly, smoked tail, and crispy ears) that is a head-to-tail tribute to Louisiana's boucherie tradition. Seafood, vegetables, wild game, and some contemporary-style sweets (chicory mocha pots de crème with coffee-infused beignets and black fig jam) round out the menu and, of course, there is a gorgeous bar where top mixologists shake up reimagined vintage cocktails or pour out a local craft beer. The culinary team has shared a dish that exemplifies our love for Louisiana's crustacean bounty and the spirit of New Orleans's Creole-Italian culinary heritage.

FAZZOLETTI & CRAWFISH PASTA

(SERVES 4)

For the crawfish stock (yields 4 cups):

1 pound crawfish heads

¼ cup roughly chopped onion

2 garlic cloves, crushed

2 tablespoons olive oil

3 lemons, thinly sliced

2 bay leaves

¼ teaspoon liquid crab boil

¾ teaspoon salt

For the fazzoletti pasta dough (yields 1 pound):

6 ounces bread flour

6¼ ounces all-purpose flour

4 eggs

1 tablespoon water

For the entree:

¼ cup crawfish stock

½ cup corn juice

2 tablespoons corn kernels

2 tablespoons olive oil

3 ounces crawfish tails

1 tablespoon butter

2 tablespoons grated Parmesan

Salt and freshly ground black pepper

3 ounces fazzoletti pasta, dry

2 fried sage leaves

Corn powder, for sprinkling

Grated orange zest, for sprinkling

To make the crawfish stock: Roast crawfish heads in a 350°F oven for 15–20 minutes. Sweat onions and garlic with a little olive oil until soft. Add remaining ingredients and 4 cups water. Simmer slowly for 20 minutes, skimming constantly. Strain.

To make the pasta: Combine ingredients in the bowl of electric mixer and mix for 5 minutes with the paddle. Wrap in plastic wrap and rest for one hour before use. Roll out using a pasta machine to number 2. Cut into 3 inch by 1½ inch rectangles.

To prepare the dish: In a large skillet, warm the crawfish stock, corn juice, corn, and olive oil. Cook corn until tender. Add the crawfish tails, butter, and Parmesan and bring to a boil, adding butter a bit at a time. Season lightly with salt and pepper to taste.

Cook pasta in boiling, salted water for 4 minutes or until tender.

Add the cooked pasta to the skillet and toss. Serve in a pasta bowl, and sprinkle the top with fried sage leaves, corn powder and orange zest.

SOBOU

310 Chartres Street
(504) 552-4095
sobounola.com

Among the Commander's Palace family of restaurants, SoBou is so named for its location south of Bourbon Street. Ti Adelaide-Martin, Alex Brennan-Martin and cousin Brad Brennan took over the space inside the W New Orleans French Quarter hotel that was once another Brennan family member's restaurant to create a "spirited restaurant." A stellar mix of food, fun and a custom cocktail list from top bar gal Amanda Thomas compliment the high style design and modern with chic lighting fixtures with sleek details like row after row of apothecary bottles in clear and frosted glass on up-lit glass shelving. Add details like a gorgeous marble-topped bar and wine menu covered in patinated copper, for a feel that is sharply cosmopolitan and new. Make no mistake, food at SoBou is in no way an afterthought or second fiddle. Chef de Cuisine Darren Porretto has ramped up the menu with a city meets country sensibility. Evidence Rustic Cajun Gumbo with smoked chicken, andouille sausage, dark roux and loads of spice; or small cones filled with tuna tartare and a wee scoop of basil and avocado ice cream. To finish, there's a decadent Bread pudding Lollipop with brandy-soaked cherries and melted white chocolate. Riffing on Commander's Shrimp & Tasso Henican SoBou serves a Shrimp & Tasso Corn Dog, but on the first Sobou menu there was a Latin vibration and these pinchos—shrimp skewered and shooting tall from a base of grilled pineapple. The drink recipe is special to this book and heavenly, a Puerto Rican rum–spiked eggnog.

SHRIMP & TASSO PINCHOS
(SERVES 8-10)

30–40 (7-inch) bamboo skewers

2 pounds 16/20-count white shrimp, peeled and deveined, tail on

1½ pounds tasso or substitute a good quality smoked ham, in large dice

Creole seasoning to taste

For the chimichurri rub (yields enough for 40 pinchos):

1 bunch flat-leaf parsley, roughly chopped

1 bunch cilantro, roughly chopped

3 ounces minced garlic

Juice of 3 lemons

1 ounce cane vinegar

16 ounces canola or vegetable oil

1 tablespoon Creole seasoning

1 teaspoon red pepper flakes

2 tablespoons salt

1 tablespoon black pepper

2 tablespoons Parmesan cheese

For the pineapple ceviche (yields 12 servings):

1½ pounds pineapple, diced

6 ounces red onion, diced

4 ounces piquillo pepper, diced

2 ounces green onion, thinly sliced

2 ounces cilantro, finely chopped

1 splash of Crystal hot sauce

Juice of 3 lemons

Juice of 2 limes

Juice of 1 orange

Salt and pepper to taste

For the pickled jalapeño pepper jelly
(yields 2½ cups):

1 cup white vinegar

1 cup cane vinegar

2 cups light Karo syrup

½ cup finely chopped pickled jalapeños

2 teaspoons sea salt

1 teaspoon black pepper

1 teaspoon red pepper flakes

1 teaspoon smoked paprika

To make the chimichurri rub: In a food processor, combine all ingredients and blend to the consistency of a wet paste.

To make the pineapple ceviche: In a large mixing bowl, combine all ingredients, toss thoroughly, and allow to rest for 40 minutes.

To make the jelly: In a large pot combine all ingredients and cook on medium-low heat to the consistency of syrup. Set aside to cool to room temperature.

To make the pinchos: Take a skewer and carefully push through the shrimp, starting from the tail end. Then take a piece of tasso and add it to the skewer. Repeat until all the shrimp are skewered. Place the pinchos on a sheet pan. Rub them with the chimichurri and let them marinate for 30 minutes. Season the pinchos with Creole seasoning and cook on the grill until the shrimp is fully cooked, about 1½ minutes on each side.

On a serving tray place the pineapple ceviche in the middle. Arrange all the shrimp pinchos around the pineapple and drizzle them with the pickled jalapeño jelly. *¡Buen provecho!*

COQUITO (PUERTO RICAN EGGNOG)

(YIELDS ABOUT 2½ QUARTS)

30 ounces Coco López or cream of coconut

12 ounces evaporated milk

14 ounces sweetened condensed milk

22 ounces Don Q Crystal white rum

¼ tablespoon ground cinnamon

¼ tablespoon ground nutmeg

1 teaspoon vanilla extract

Mix all ingredients in a blender on high speed. Refrigerate. Make sure to shake well before serving. Serve cold, sip, and enjoy.

STANLEY

547 Saint Ann Street
(504) 587-0093
stanleyrestaurant.com

Chef Scott Boswell's French Quarter casual coffee shop featuring deep, dark seafood-and-sausage-studded gumbo, Eggs Benedict Poor Boys, fried oysters or soft shell crab with poached eggs, a tall beefy Reuben, and the Stanley Burger, continues strong with its upscale diner fare, and an expanded menu to include a few specialty po-boys, a soda shop complete with ice cream, shakes, and malts; and a full bar with adult beverages including an Irish Coffee milkshake that punches with Irish whiskey. Cajun Spiced Ribs, a funny, boozy concoction he calls a Screamer and, and, and. Chef Scott knows no boundaries. This recipe for Stanley's Omelet Sandwich (still on the menu) was among the favorites devoured by those who ate at the first Stanley on Decatur Street, during those strange, desolate post Hurricane Katrina days of late September 2005.

OMELET SANDWICH

(SERVES 1)

1 tablespoon butter, divided

1 ounce onions, sliced thick

1 ounce mayonnaise

Pinch of cayenne

2 ounces smoked ham, chopped

1 ounce bacon, chopped

½ ounce green onions, chopped

2–3 eggs

Salt and pepper to taste

2 slices American cheese

2 slices 9-grain bread

To caramelize the onions: On high heat, melt ½ tablespoon of butter in a nonstick frying pan. Add onions and stir frequently until golden brown. Set aside.

To make the spicy mayonnaise: Mix mayonnaise and cayenne pepper thoroughly.

To prepare the omelet: Melt ½ teaspoon of butter into a 6 inch, non-stick frying pan on medium heat. Add caramelized onions, smoked ham, chopped bacon and green onions and mix until all ingredients are coated in warmed butter.

Crack 2–3 eggs into bowl and add salt and pepper. Whisk vigorously. Add eggs to pan and gently stir until ingredients are evenly distributed. Allow to cook for about 1 minute, until the bottom of the eggs has set without coloring. With a heat-resistant rubber spatula, gently flip the omelet over and allow to cook for another 30 seconds, or until eggs are fully cooked. Fold omelet in half, add both slices of American cheese to top, and allow to melt in broiler.

To assemble: Brush butter on each side of 9-grain bread and toast, then add spicy mayonnaise to each slice. Once cheese has melted on omelet, place on bread and close the sandwich.

DEL FUEGO

4518 Magazine Street
(504) 309-5797
delfuegotaqueria.com

Chef David Wright (AKA "Fine Dining Dave") is a Baja California boy and Shannon Solomon Wright, his wife is a Louisiana gal. Both of them are industry powerhouses with big love for Mexican culture, cuisine and tequila. Their restaurant, Del Fuego is a casual taqueria mid-block on a busy stretch of Magazine Street, just a bit uptown from Napoleon Avenue where many parades line up for Mardi Gras. The corn tortillas are made on site, the salsas range from mild to on-fire, and the fantastic margaritas blend fresh-squeezed juices with sturdy shots of tequila. The menu is a fascinating blend of California, Mexico and Louisiana, showcasing local seafood, meats, rice, beans and vegetables for tacos, or to be tucked into big flour tortillas for massive burritos. Pulling from a deep love of Mexican street food, there is roasted corn on the cob (Eloté) striped with chipotle mayo, spices, chopped cilantro, crumbled cotija cheese and squeezes of fresh lime juice; and a bacon-wrapped loaded Sonoran hot dog to devour. Speaking of "loaded," their chunky guacamole comes topped with pickled onions, bacon bits, poblano peppers, tomato, jalapeños and fried pork skins (chicharrones). Dave and Shannon have fun at their restaurant and they work hard.

They're great community partners too, holding bingo parties and special dinners to fund-raise for worthy organizations. Of all the salsas, I'm nuts for the rich, pumpkin seed dip called "Sikil Pak." I put it on everything, sometimes casuing Chef Dave to shake his head. Dave and Shannon graciously shared their recipe and this tid-bit about sikil pak: "A staple in the Yucatan, it is delicious eaten with tortilla chips and raw vegetables, and it can also be used as a sauce for chicken, fish or pork, a salsa for tacos and burritos, or a spread for sandwiches. The uses are endless."

SEARED YELLOWFIN TUNA TOSTADA

(MAKES 8 TOSTADAS)

1½ lbs. sushi grade yellowfin tuna, cut into 6-8 inch "loins" approximately 2 inches in diameter

1 pint guacamole, homemade or your favorite store brand

1 cup serrano-pineapple vinaigrette (recipe follows)

2 ears of corn, fresh in the husk

½ of a medium red onion, medium diced

1 cup grape tomatoes, halved

1 cup black beans, cooked whole and rinsed thoroughly (canned will suffice)

1 serrano chili, sliced thinly

¼ cup chopped cilantro

8 tostadas (can be purchased fresh at your local tortilleria)

½ cup toasted pepitas, seasoned with salt and chili powder

For the Serrano-Pineapple Vinaigrette (approximately 1½ cups)

1 serrano chili (seeded if you don't want the heat)

⅓ cup lime juice

2 tablespoon pineapple juice

1 tablespoon agave nectar

1 teaspoon Dijon mustard

2 tablespoon cilantro, chopped

1 cup salad oil

Salt to taste

To prepare the tuna: Preheat a cast iron skillet or sauté pan on medium high heat. Season tuna loins liberally with salt, cracked black pepper and chili powder. Add a small amount of oil to the pan, it should be on the verge of smoking. Sear each side of the loins for 25–30 seconds. If it has a bit of a blackened look that is just fine. Tuna should still be completely raw in the middle unless you prefer it otherwise. Put into refrigerator until it is time to use. This can be done, 2–3 hours ahead of time.

To prepare the corn salad: Cook corn in the oven with husks still on for 35 minutes, allow to cool. Shuck corn and char over an open flame (gas stove flame is fine), this step can be skipped if you have an electric stove. Remove kernels from cob and dispose of cobs. Add black beans, corn, tomatoes, red onion, serrano chili and cilantro to a small bowl and mix. Add 2 tablespoons of the vinaigrette and a couple pinches of salt and mix again.

Vinaigrette: Add all ingredients except oil to blender and blend for 20 seconds or so. Slowly add oil until emulsified.

Season with salt.

To plate: For each tostada, layer as follows. Place a small dollop of guacamole on the plate, then the tostada.

Smear another heaping tablespoon of guacamole, then spoon 3 or so heaping tablespoons of corn salad making sure the tomatoes get distributed evenly. With a sharp knife slice the tuna into ⅓ inch slices, 16 slices total. Arrange 2 slices of tuna onto each tostada. Sprinkle the pepitas and drizzle vinaigrette onto the tuna and around each plate. Enjoy!

SIKIL PAK

MAKES ABOUT 1½ QUARTS

1 ripe tomato

½ medium yellow onion

1 habanero, stemmed

3 cloves of garlic

¼ cup of orange juice

2 tablespoon lime juice

3 green onions, roughly chopped

1 cup pepitas, toasted

½ cup cilantro, chopped

Water

Salt

Heat oven to 500°F. Roast tomato, onion, garlic and habanero for 8–10 minutes. Add roasted ingredients, lime juice, orange juice and green onions to blender. Blend until completely liquefied. Add pepitas and continue to blend. The mixture will thicken quickly. You will need to gradually add enough water so that the mixture will continue to spin around the blades. Continue blending until totally smooth, add small amounts of water if necessary. The finished mixture should be the consistency of ketchup. Season with salt and chopped cilantro.

A MUFFULETTA NAMED DESIRE

Mikko is a culture, theatre, and history buff who has shared a foodie version of Tennessee Williams's *A Streetcar Named Desire* reimagined by him and his fellow writer Lisa McCaffety. Beloved local chef Anthony Spizale, a local guy of Creole Italian heritage, makes some of the best olive salad and, in typical fashion, came up with a creative Muffuletta Hand Pie recipe to go along with Mikko and Lisa's "book."

A MODEST FRENCH QUARTER HOME.

There is a hubbub of four men, Stanley, Mitch, Pablo, and Steve, and a woman, Stella, scurrying around the kitchen. They are all preparing food for an upcoming affair. Stella moves with an unassuming flair that threatens neither women nor the men that want to be women. Stanley chops olives with a virility rarely seen in the musky, husky vapors of the swamps commonly found around the decaying and decadent crescent that is the city known as New Orleans. The other men are not attractive to me; I will say a few more things about Stanley: He is carnal in his manners, there is the touch of the animal in him as if any moment he will prepare a country-style gazpacho and not use any oregano. His leering, muscular innuendo propels the project in the kitchen—women and men around him sense the audacity of his Viking-like chopping. He— Excuse me? Well, I am starting the play . . . Pardon? This is necessary for me to lay the scene . . . What? . . . Do you know I am friends with Liz Taylor and Anna Magnani? . . . But Paul Newman said . . . Oh very well! (Sigh) . . .

Polka music plays in the background. . . . Bitch.

STANLEY   Hey Stella!

STELLA   Whatcha yellin' for, Stanley? I'm right here.

STANLEY   Meat!

Throws a packet of deli meat to her, but she is so close it sails over her head and crashes into the spice rack.

MITCH   Hey Stanley, how do you convert from teaspoons to metric?

STANLEY   Whatcha lookin' at metric for? What are ya, some kind of swishy lavender European?

MITCH   What's wrong with European? That's the old country, ain't it?

STANLEY   Look, can it. My family came to America to be in America. This is the land of the free. And you, Pablo, put down those carrots, I ain't lettin' no beaner touch my olive salad.

During this exchange, a slight but radiant woman enters unseen. She is shy, but with a trace of coquettishness that is attractive only when found in wispy females that portend or pretend nobility. There is the sense of a moth about her, as if she would dash herself to perdition against the dangerous lightbulbs of society's useless mores. She might even be mistaken for a butterfly and in certain parts of the world, even this rutting and rotting village in the marshes of the Mississippi delta, a delicate hummingbird that passes from sweet and forbidden flower to another damning— Pardon? I would remind you that Gore Vidal once confided in me . . . Who is Gore Vidal? Now, Truman, you are crossing the line . . . but . . . but . . . (Sigh) Fine.

The polka music settles into a plaintive tuba in a minor key.

BLANCHE   I was told to take a streetcar named "Desire" then transfer to the "Cemeteries" bus and then get off at Elysian Fields.

STANLEY   (*Barking at her*) It ain't a streetcar no more.

BLANCHE   Oh, I apologize, I . . .

MITCH	(Soothingly approaches her.) That's all right, Ma'am. He means that "Desire" is a bus now, not a streetcar.
BLANCHE	That explains my forty-seven-block promenade from the Greyhound station.
MITCH	(Smiling) You sure don't look like you walked forty-seven blocks.
STANLEY	Mitch! Get over here and chop this celery!
BLANCHE	Oh, you are a chef de cuisine?
MITCH	Nah, we all just get together and make New Orleans specialties.
STANLEY	(Coming over with a bunch of celery, interrupting.) I'm gonna make a special New Orleans punch on the side of your head if you don't get over to that chopping board.

He tosses the bunch of celery back to the work area in the kitchen, where it smashes into a group of empty beer bottles on top of the refrigerator.

	You must be Stella's big sister.
BLANCHE	(Her retiring demeanor drops and she embodies a beaming charm.) Younger sister, actually, but I forgive you, for my sister eternally channels the vitality and allure of Aphrodite.
STANLEY	Mm-hmm. What do you think about canola oil?

continued . . .

MUFFULETTA HAND PIE

(MAKES 20 HAND PIES)

4 ounces mortadella

4 ounces Genoa salami

4 ounces prosciutto

1 pound provolone

2 ounces grated Parmigiano-Reggiano

1 cup plus 1 tablespoon extra-virgin olive oil

½ cup green olives, pitted

½ cup kalamata or other black olives, pitted

2 ounces capers

1 celery rib, thinly sliced

1 teaspoon garlic, finely chopped

1 small carrot, peeled and diced

1 roasted red pepper, diced

1 bunch green onions, sliced

3 tablespoons red wine vinegar

2 tablespoons dried oregano

6 fresh basil leaves, torn

1 teaspoon Italian parsley, finely chopped

1 teaspoon crushed red pepper flakes

Kosher salt and freshly ground pepper, to taste

1 (14-ounce) package dough disks for empanadas

Vegetable oil, for frying

2 ounces sesame seeds

Cut the three meats and the provolone in small dice. Toss in a bowl with the grated Parmigiano-Reggiano and 1 tablespoon olive oil. Set aside.

Combine green olives, black olives, and capers in a large stainless steel bowl. Crush the olives and capers with your hands. Add the celery, garlic, carrots, roasted peppers, and green onions. Toss together lightly.

Combine red wine vinegar with 1 cup olive oil, dried oregano, basil, parsley, and red pepper flakes. Season to taste with salt and pepper. Blend well. Add to the meat-cheese mixture and toss together lightly with the olive salad. Cover and refrigerate 2–3 hours.

Lay out empanada disks on a floured work table. Spoon about 1 tablespoon of meat and olive mixture into the middle of one disk. Fold in half to form a half moon; moisten edges with water and pinch to close, or seal with a fork. Repeat for the rest of the dough disks.

Fill a deep saucepan with oil to a depth of 2½ inches. Heat oil over medium-high heat until hot but not smoking, 350°F on deep-fry thermometer. Cook empanadas in batches, flipping once, until crisp and golden brown, 4–6 minutes. Transfer to paper towels to drain, and sprinkle with sesame seeds.

BLANCHE   Oh, Mr. Kowalski, I disdain it. And except for that Italian elixir from the fruit of the olive tree, I eschew all oils as I would a crass remark or a vulgar gesture.

STANLEY   STELLA!

BLANCHE   *(This ejaculation has unnerved her. She reaches into her purse for a cigarette.)* Yes, where is my lovely sister?

STANLEY   *(Indicating her purse.)* You got any Vidalia onions in there?

BLANCHE   Why, no . . .

STELLA   *(Entering.)* Oh, Blanche, my darling baby, how was your trip? I'm so glad to see you. I hope Stanley has been making you feel welcome.

Stanley grunts, and goes back to his work.

STELLA   Let's go in the other room and catch up.

They enter another part of the house where Blanche starts to unpack her things.

STELLA   Would you like a nice lemon Coke to cool you down, baby?

BLANCHE   Oh, my angelic sister, as the poet said, "My soul thirsteth . . ."

Stella goes back into the kitchen to prepare the drink. Stanley pulls her aside. Blanche turns the television on. The polka music becomes accusatory and insinuating.

STANLEY   Listen, baby, you think she brought any with her?

STELLA   Any what? Honest to God, Stanley, the poor girl has had a hard trip and you want to bother her with silly things.

STANLEY: It ain't so silly. What they got here in Louisiana is what you call your Muffuletta Code. In the Muffuletta Code it says that Vidalia onions are the best for a great olive salad. Vidalia onions grow best in Mississippi, and your sister is from Mississippi.
(To Blanche in the other room.) Quiet down that racket!

STELLA: You know, Stanley, you should pay more attention to your salami.

She returns to her sister with the drink.

MITCH: Your sister-in-law is a charming girl.

STANLEY: Listen, I got an acquaintance friend of mine that is a salesman. He has occasion to travel through Laurel, Mississippi, a lot, and he tells me there is this blonde fancy-pants that is known as the Vidalia Queen.

MITCH: *(Getting angry)* Now just stop right there! You don't know everything, you know!

Mitch storms out of the kitchen into the dark and uncertain night.

STANLEY: *(To the ladies in the other room.)* You two cut out that racket!

He storms into the other room. The two ladies are watching Emeril on TV. We hear Emeril:

EMERIL (O.S.) . . . Sprinkle a few jimmies on the chocolate and Bam! (Or whatever it is Emeril says) we got a delicious doughnut! (We hear the audience clapping) Now that my friends, is a doughnut! . . .

STANLEY: *(Throwing the TV out of the window.)* Cut the re-bop!out of the window.) Cut the re-bop!

Stella is so upset she storms out of the room into the disquieting safety of night.

BLANCHE: *(Frightened.)* I am not afraid of you.

STANLEY: *(Approaching her)* What we got here in Louisiana is the Muffuletta Code . . .

BLANCHE: I don't know your brand of Italian, Mr. Kowalski, the only Italian I know is the strains of Verdi, Puccini . . .

Stanley grabs her purse and tears it apart. As he continues to root through her many bags, she dissolves into that state that many true artists and very few people who have not lived in the French Quarter understand.

BLANCHE: Puccini, that's right. Tosca, who is set upon by the beast of a man Scarpia. She pleads with him, in the way I plead with you. Vissi d'Arte! Vissi d'arte!

Stanley has found a travel bag, and as he rips the zipper open, dozens of Vidalia onions tumble out onto the floor. Blanche swoons to the daybed.

BLANCHE: *(continued)* Yes! I have lived for art! Yes! I have lived for Vidalia onions!

Blanche collapses spent to the couch. Stanley drops to his knees in ecstasy, throwing the Vidalia onions into the air above him. He rejoices. The polka shifts into a somber indictment of masculinity.

STANLEY: Stella! Stella!!! HEY, STELLA!!!!!

Curtain.

SYLVAIN

625 Chartres Street
(504) 265-8123
sylvainnola.com

In a space that was once a fabulous French bakery just off Jackson Square, Sylvain is a dark, pub-like sort of place, all dark wood, leather-topped stools, and low lighting. Take the narrow walkway onto the courtyard where the slave-quarter-housed kitchen is immediately visible. A sharp left through the French doors leads to the hostess station and bar and, just beyond that, a handful of tables that face Chartres Street. Sylvain's menu of crafty cocktails stirred by dedicated mixologists, and even craftier food by newly ensconced Kyle Coppinger who is breathing some new life into the menu while retaining some of the spirit created by the original chef. The food and drink excel at being both deeply flavored thought simple and with few ingredients. Sylvain remains a cool yet brawny French Quarter gastropub. The Chicken Sandwich once called cheekily called the Chick-Syl-vain is still an item, though it now sits shoulder-to-shoulder with Braised Beef Cheeks, Creole Ratatouille, and fresh-made Pappardelle with Bolognese. This is a happy marriage of old world vibes and modern food and drinks, has undeniable longevity.

PICKLED GULF SHRIMP WITH LOCAL TOMATOES, BUTTER BEANS, SPROUTS & GREEN GODDESS DRESSING

(SERVES 4 AS APPETIZER, 2 AS ENTREE)

For the shrimp boil:

1 teaspoon yellow mustard seeds

1 teaspoon coriander seeds

3 bay leaves

1 teaspoon whole black peppercorns

1 teaspoon red pepper flakes

1 lemon, cut in half

½ tablespoon white wine vinegar

4 whole garlic cloves, crushed

1 tablespoon sea salt or kosher salt

For the pickled Gulf shrimp:

1 pound Gulf shrimp

2 quarts shrimp boil

1 cup extra virgin olive oil

¼ cup freshly squeezed lemon juice

1 medium yellow onion, thinly sliced

4 crushed garlic cloves

½ teaspoon ground celery seeds

½ teaspoon red pepper flakes

½ teaspoon yellow mustard seeds

½ teaspoon coriander seeds

6 bay leaves

For the Green Goddess Dressing:

1 teaspoon chopped anchovies

1 tablespoon chopped chives

1 tablespoon chopped tarragon

½ tablespoon chopped basil

¼ cup chopped flat-leaf parsley

½ teaspoon minced garlic

½ cup mayonnaise

¼ cup buttermilk

1 teaspoon lemon juice

1 tablespoon apple cider vinegar

Pinch of kosher salt

Black pepper to taste

For the salad:

1 pound pickled Gulf shrimp

2 ripe tomatoes, sliced

1 cup butter beans, blanched in salted water

1 ounce sprouts—sunflower, pea, radish

Salt and pepper

½ tablespoon extra virgin olive oil

6 ounces Green Goddess Dressing

To make the shrimp boil: Combine all ingredients in a large sauce pot with 2 quarts water and bring to a boil over medium-high heat. Reduce the heat and simmer the liquid for 5 minutes.

To make the pickled Gulf shrimp: Cook the shrimp in the boil until they have started to turn pink, about 2 minutes. Place the oil, lemon juice, onion, garlic, and herbs and spices in a mixing bowl and whisk to combine. Toss the shrimp with this pickling mixture and place in a nonreactive container. Refrigerate for at least 1 hour before serving. The shrimp will keep for 3 days under refrigeration.

To make the Green Goddess Dressing: Place all the ingredients in a food processor or blender and process until smooth and green, about 30 seconds. Adjust salt and pepper to taste.

To make the salad: Toss the pickled Gulf shrimp, tomatoes, butter beans, and sprouts with salt, pepper, and extra virgin olive oil. Divide half of the Green Goddess Dressing between 2 or 4 plates. Place even amounts of shrimp and tomato mixture on the plates. Drizzle the plates with the remaining Green Goddess Dressing.

BITTERSWEET CONFECTIONS

725 Magazine Street
(504) 523-2626
bittersweetconfections.com

New Orleans first tasted Cheryl Scripter's nobby handmade chocolate truffles when she rolled them out at the Crescent City Farmers Market in 2001—deep, dark high quality, sometimes left plain, sometimes flavored with essences or spices and then tumbled in cocoa powder, bright fruit powders, or crisp croquantes. Cheryl tutored sweets eaters in the art of chocolate, and the city was addicted. Evolving her chocolate selection to include special collections with a local beat, Bittersweet Confections literally melted hearts. Suddenly there were more confections, cakes, chocolate-dipped fruits, and a slew of lovely chocolaty treats. Cheryl's shop on Magazine Street now has sisters—a free-standing spot in New Orleans Lakeview area and another in Marigny food hall, St. Roch Market. Cheryl and her baking, confection-making crew continue to truffle, but they also fashion nonpareils, dip caramels, and cluster coconut in chocolate. They bake big, delectable King Cakes, fun-flavored cupcakes, killer cookies, chewy brownies; the list is endless. In short, there is a bit of chocolate confection heaven right here in the Crescent City, and it's Bittersweet . . . for those minding their waistlines.

BITTERSWEET CONFECTION MARSHMALLOWS

(YIELDS 32 MARSHMALLOWS)

2¼ cups 10X sugar

2¼ cups cornstarch

Nonstick cooking spray

4½ cups granulated sugar

1½ cups white corn syrup

2¼ cups cold water

¾ teaspoon salt

1½ ounces gelatin

3 tablespoons pure vanilla extract

10 ounces chocolate, 58% cacao

4 ounces graham crackers

Sift the 10X sugar with the cornstarch into a small bowl. Spray two 9 x 9 x 2-inch baking pans with nonstick spray and coat with ⅓ cup of the powdered sugar–cornstarch mixture. Set aside.

In a medium heavy-bottomed pot, stir together the granulated sugar, corn syrup, 1½ cups water, and the salt. Bring to a boil over medium to medium-high heat and continue to cook until the temperature reaches 236°F.

Meanwhile, fill a medium bowl with remaining water and add ice. When syrup mixture reaches 236°F, remove the syrup pan from the heat and dip the bottom in the ice water for about 5 seconds to lower the temperature.

While waiting for the syrup to cool, put gelatin into the work-bowl of a stand mixer. When the syrup is

down to 210°F, pour it into the gelatin and stir to combine. Mix at medium-high speed for 5–7 minutes, or until thick and fluffy. Add the vanilla and whip for another 30 seconds.

Spray a spatula with nonstick spray and scrape the marshmallow cream into the prepared pans. Sprinkle the remaining 10X-sugar-and-cornstarch mixture over the top of the cream. Let stand overnight.

Cut into squares. Temper 10 ounces of chocolate and finely crush 4 ounces of graham crackers. Dip each square into the chocolate and roll in the crumbs.

CLANCY'S

6100 Annunciation Street
(504) 895-1111
clancysneworleans.com

This elegant, yet comfortable restaurant sits deep in a residential neighborhood near Audubon Park. Though Clancy's doesn't have the age of the "grand dames," it *feels* old, in the best way possible. Tuxedoed waiters suggest formality but it's a trick of the eye as they share easy, sometimes bawdy banter with regulars and guests. Clancy's is not only an outstanding local dining go-to, it's a great place to take visitors. The menus are handwritten in a fine slanted script hand and include starters standards like oysters and brie, fried eggplant and aioli; and seafood gumbo. From the entrees, take note of the smoked soft shell crab with

roasted garlic meuniere; sautéed Gulf fish, a tender filet with Stilton and a red wine demi-glace. By the way, everything, I mean everything can be lushly topped with local lump crabmeat. In fact crabmeat is almost a requirement at Clancy's. Every meal should begin with marinated crab claws and end with Clancy's insanely good lemon Icebox Pie. Luckily Chef-Proprietor Brian Larsen agreed to share these classic recipes.

CLANCY'S LOUISIANA CRAB CLAWS WITH CILANTRO AND LIME

2 cups fresh squeezed lime juice

2 cups rice wine vinegar

¼ cup canola oil

1 teaspoon sambal chili paste

1 green bell pepper, finely diced

1 red bell pepper, finely diced

1 jalapeño pepper, finely diced

1 bunch green onions, small chop

1 bunch cilantro, chopped

Combine all ingredients in a bowl and add 2 lbs. fresh Louisiana Crab Claws and marinate for a minimum of 30 minutes. Serve Chilled.

LEMON ICEBOX PIE

(MAKES 2, 14 INCH PIES)

12 egg yolks

4 cups freshly squeezed lemon juice

6 12-ounce cans sweetened condensed milk

2 14-inch graham cracker pie crusts*

Note: We make our own crusts, but a store bought crust will work well.

Whisk together condensed milk and lemon juice in a mixing bowl. Be sure to taste the mixture for a balance of sweet and tart. You want the mixture to be slightly more tart. If more lemon juice is needed, add until desired flavor is reached. Slowly whisk in egg yolks and mix thoroughly. Pour mixture into pie shells with a ¼ inch of pie shell showing. Bake Pies at 300°F for 20 minutes.

Freeze pies for 24 hours so pie completely sets. Top with whipped cream and serve.

DELGADO COMMUNITY COLLEGE CULINARY SCHOOL

615 City Park Avenue
(504) 671-6199
www.dcc.edu

Several years ago, I was honored to be asked to teach Food Writing and Culinary Social Media at New Orleans's oldest (100 years in 2021!) Community College, Delgado. The experience has been life-changing. I never knew how much I'd enjoy the classroom, students and teaching . . . I do now! Cliche though it may be, I honestly find learning a two-way street and I definitely get an education from my students; I love them all, a ton. I'm a true believer in the community college system as a game-changer to education and life. I'm so proud to be among the change-agent educators at Delgado—they are a brilliant team of people. The Culinary Program is incredible with top-notch full-time instructors of diverse backgrounds and experiences. We're a food-cooking-hospitality nerd herd doing delicious and extraordinary things to help educate and prepare students for entering a wide range of culinary and hospitality jobs. My particular role in the program is a bit unusual, and a perfect fit. Not many culinary schools offer a course in Social Media, but Delgado saw this as mission critical because today, it is imperative for chefs to know how to navigate social media. The class also provides the opportunity to discuss food, family, culture, community, race, philanthropy, causes, photography, history and etiquette. Yep, we go there.

Many, many thanks to Delgado Community College and the stellar team in Culinary & Hospitality for giving me (and our students) the opportunity to be in your company, to learn from you, and for the incentive, sometimes firm push, we all need on the daily.

"No crying in the walk-in!"

In lab classes, where the students learn technical culinary skills, a lot of cooking ground is covered. Other cultures' food notwithstanding, the subject of New Orleans specific cuisine always bubbles up. Yes, gumbo, that great, sturdy soup with a million versions and just as many possible ingredients, is fiercely and lovingly debated. Who makes the best gumbo? Your family.

The recipe below is from the hands of the supreme jokester and excellent cook, Chef Lou. I first tasted his gumbo at an on-campus event and it has never left my thoughts. Lou graciously agreed to not only share the recipe, but pared it down from the massive quantities he makes, to a reasonable version for home cooks. You da best, Lou!

GUMBO

(SERVES 6-8)

⅔ cup canola oil

⅔ cup flour

⅔ cup chopped onion

⅓ cup chopped green bell pepper

⅓ cup chopped celery

2 tablespoons minced garlic

2 tablespoons file powder

1 gallon crab stock OR shrimp stock OR a combination

1 tablespoon liquid crab boil (more or less depending on your taste)

2 teaspoon dried thyme

2 teaspoon dried oregano

1 cup chopped tomato

3 tablespoon shrimp base

1 tablespoon Kitchen Bouquet® (more or less depending on your color preference)

2 cups frozen sliced okra

1 pound shrimp

1 pound crawfish tails

1 pound crabmeat OR ½ pound each crabmeat and cocktail claws

¼ cup chopped parsley

⅔ cup sliced green onion

Heat oil and whisk in flour. Cook about 20 minutes, whisking almost constantly until the roux is slightly lighter than chocolate.

Remove from heat and stir in onion, pepper and celery. Mix well. Wait 5 minutes and add the garlic and file powder. Mix well again. The 5 minute delay will ensure that the garlic and file won't burn.

Chill well. I find it best to make this a day ahead.

In a large pot, heat stock or water.

Add okra, thyme, oregano, tomato, and shrimp base.

When stock boils, reduce heat and begin whisking in roux/vegetable mixture about a tennis ball sized piece at a time, crumbling it as you add.

After each addition, whisk well to distribute the roux and let cook about 5 minutes.

Keep adding roux until the desired thickness is reached.

Set heat to medium low, and let simmer about 30 minutes, stirring and skimming the surface of impurities as needed. Kitchen Bouquet can be added at this point, if desired.

Check seasoning and adjust with oregano, thyme, salt and pepper if necessary.

Add seafood, parsley and green onion. Return to a simmer. Stir well, turn off heat, cover and let stand for 10 minutes. This will ensure that the seafood does not overcook.

MAYHEW BAKERY

3201 Orleans Avenue
(843) 814-3020
facebook.com/mayhewbakery

Kelly Mayhew is the most unlikely of bakers. A former US Army Infantry-man, with three tours behind him and a rather ugly (he shows it) service-related leg wound, he was at a loss for next steps—no pun intended. He decided to enroll in culinary school at The Art Institute of Charleston, South Carolina and he's hardwired for the profession (fun fact: Kelly's family opened the first Krispy Kreme franchise). Fierce and intense he started his career in cuisine as Sous Chef at Brennan's, ultimately becoming corporate baker for the restaurant. He then began selling his baked goods at the Crescent City Farmers' Market and made enough to open a teeny, tiny shop. Actually it was a former snowball stand and he sold baked goods through a window. I've spent many hours in Chef Kelly's bakery kitchen and am always awed. His dark, crackly-crusted baguettes have a stunningly light crumb, scones are properly crumbly, canales creamy, and buttery croissants dreamy. Kelly and I gnashed our teeth about what recipe he might share. We decided that when it comes to baking, everyone needs a great cookie in their repertoire and this one is gorgeous, especially for its simplicity and flexibility—alter the extracts to alter the flavor, or don't. This is a keeper, as is.

SUGAR COOKIE

¾ pound butter, room temp

¾ pound sugar

2 ounces sour cream

2 eggs

½ teaspoon vanilla extract

⅛ teaspoon almond extract

¼ teaspoon lemon oil or extract

Zest of 1 lemon

1¼ pounds all purpose flour

1½ teaspoons baking powder

½ teaspoon baking soda

1 teaspoon salt

Raw sugar crystals for decorating

In a stand mixer with the paddle attachment, cream the butter at low speed with the sugar, salt, and extracts. How long you cream depends on whether you want a lighter or more dense cookie. Longer creaming makes cookies lighter. Less creaming makes them spread less and be chewier. Add the eggs, sour cream and lemon zest, blending to combine. Sift in the flour, baking soda and baking powder. Mix until combined. Using a #16 (2 ounce) scoop, form cookie dough balls. Roll the balls in large crystal raw sugar and bake on parchment-lined baking sheets for approximately 16 minutes or until edges are light brown.

DOMENICA

123 Baronne Street
(504) 648-6020
domenicarestaurant.com

At the edge of New Orleans Central Business District, just across Canal Street from the French Quarter is the ornate and elegant old world, Roosevelt Hotel. Domenica a sleek, contemporarily designed space of dark brown walls, chain-mail curtains, and giant brightly colored paintings. The menu of rustic Italian dishes, pizzas, pastas, salumi, and savory beignets. Here, the roasted cauliflower with whipped feta, has have a crazy cult following by even the most ardent of carnivores. It is simply stunning thing: a whole head of cauliflower, olive oil poached and roasted til tender and burnished. The specially built pizza oven bakes up beautifully bubbled, slightly charred pies topped with house-made salumi, market vegetables, cheeses, and spices. Making a meal of a pizza, a vegetable side, and a bottle of wine from the well-curated list is the way most diners go, if they can pass up the big salumi and condiments board. Domenica gets creative with special coursed dinners held throughout the year and is packed for the half-price pizza Happy Hour. There are house-crafted fruit and herb cellos, cocktails, and joyful desserts like the Chocolate-Hazelnut Budino or seasonal fruit cobblers. Re-creating Domenica's pizzas takes skill and a wood-fired pizza oven, so they shared one of the excellent pasta recipes with an earthy tender pork ragù.

HANDMADE PASTA WITH MANGALITSA PORK RAGÙ

This is a dish reminiscent of a "family meal" in Italy. Halfway through the workday, people often stop and sit down to lunch together taking time to cherish a meal and great conversation.

(SERVES 6)

For the pasta:

10 ounces pasta flour, number 00

8 ounces ricotta

2 eggs

Salt to taste

Pinch of freshly grated nutmeg

For the ragù:

2 pounds bone-in shoulder of pork, preferably Mangalitsa

1 tablespoon kosher salt

1 teaspoon ground black pepper

¼ cup olive oil

¼ onion, chopped fine

1 carrot, peeled and chopped fine

2 stalks celery, chopped fine

1 clove garlic, chopped fine

1 cup peeled, cored, and diced tomatoes

1 cup dry red wine

1 quart water

¼ teaspoon ground cloves

½ teaspoon ground nutmeg

8 black peppercorns

2 sprigs rosemary

1 sprig oregano

2 bay leaves

For assembly:

2 tablespoons salt

6 cups pasta

2 tablespoons olive oil

2 cups pork ragù

1 cup good-quality tomato sauce

3 cups Tuscan kale, cleaned and ripped into large
pieces

4 tablespoons dried red currants, reconstituted in
pork broth

3 tablespoons cold unsalted butter

6 tablespoons grated Parmigiano-Reggiano

2 tablespoons extra virgin olive oil, for finishing

To make the pasta: Place flour on a wooden table or cutting board and make a well in the middle with your fingers. Add the ricotta, eggs, salt, and nutmeg to the middle. Using a fork, begin to work the wet ingredients into the dry ingredients until they all come together and form a dough. Knead the dough with your hands for about 8–10 minutes or until it looks smooth. Sprinkle a touch more flour on the work surface if the dough begins to stick. Let dough rest for 1 hour.

Using a rolling pin, roll out the dough in a large rectangle until it is ¼ inch thick. Using a pizza cutter, cut lengthwise into ½-inch strips. Then cut 1½-inch segments from each strip. You should now have rectangular pieces that are ¼ x ½ x 1½ inches. With your thumb, press each rectangle onto a gnocchi board and roll with a downward motion to form a hollow tube with the pasta so that the pasta curls over onto itself. If you don't have a gnocchi board, you can just press it on a wooden cutting board.

Once you have a good quantity made, dust with flour and place in a single layer on a baking sheet. Then you can wrap and freeze for future use.

To prepare the pork ragù: Preheat oven to 325 F. Season the pork shoulder with salt and pepper. In a large saucepan or Dutch oven, place the olive oil on high heat and wait until it begins to smoke. Add the seasoned pork. Reduce heat to medium. Brown the pork on all sides. Remove from the pan. Add the onion, carrot, celery, and garlic and cook over medium heat until golden brown. Add the tomatoes and wine and simmer until the wine reduces by half. Add the water, clove, nutmeg, peppercorns, rosemary, oregano, and bay leaves. Place the pork back in the pot. The liquid should barely cover the meat. Bring to a simmer and cover the pot.

Place in the oven for 2–3 hours or until tender. Allow to cool, then remove pork from the broth and pull all the meat off the bones. Cut meat into small pieces and return to the broth. (This can be done 2 days ahead.)

To assemble: In a large pot, bring 1 gallon of water and 2 tablespoons of salt to a rolling boil. Add the pasta and cook for 5–7 minutes until tender.

Meanwhile, heat a large sauté pan over medium heat. Place 2 tablespoons olive oil in the pan and heat until very hot. Add pork ragù, tomato sauce, kale, and currants. Simmer until the liquid in the pan has reduced by half. Add the pasta to the sauté pan and simmer until the sauce reduces and coats the pasta. Add the butter and the grated cheese. Taste for seasoning. After you plate the dish, sprinkle 2 tablespoons of very good extra virgin olive oil over it.

WEST BANK STORY: GO WEST(BANK)
A CULINARY CULTURAL EXPLORATION
OF THE "OTHER SIDE OF THE RIVER"

It's like gumbo. Cliché though it may be, there is frank truth to the metaphor: New Orleans is a diverse collection of cultures and people, deliciously stirred together.

Head east across the curvy Mississippi to the "Westbank" (so called for being situated on the river's west bank) for more local stew, both old and new(ish). Neighborhoods like Algiers Point, Gretna and Westwego are historic, filled with families of traditional Louisiana roots (French, Spanish, African, Italian and German), as well as those with ties to Vietnam and the Middle East. In a rather old-fashioned way, there is a beautiful heritage story told through markets, cooks and food makers. It's as easy as a ferry ride or car hop across the Crescent City Connection bridge; plan to fill up on New Orleans' Westbank food and culture.

A quick, four-mile trek from the Westbank side of bridge means chasing a broad expanse of cement and sky on the high-rise portion of the expressway. Big-box stores and crowded commercial strip centers give way to open spaces and circling gulls, looping and dipping over the Westwego Seafood Lot. Turn into the shell-and-gravel parking lot flanked by rows of uniquely decorated stalls of family-owned and -run seafood businesses.

On display is the day's catch—big cooler chests filled with layers of ice and fresh-caught seasonal fin fish, shrimp, crab, squid, frog legs, crawfish and more. The vendors, often clad in shorts

and white rubber "shrimp boots," are from families that have fished the surrounding waters forever. Scooping giant shrimp into scale baskets for weighing and bagging, or wrapping seafood in fat rolls of newspaper, there's plenty of chatter and cooking advice; food conversation is the same as breathing air.

Back on the expressway, exit at 6B, and turn right on Scottsdale Drive to hit a covered, open-air market called the Westbank Flea Market. This is no regular flea-market affair; the centerpiece is a covered-yet-open food hall of individually decorated stalls, complete with electricity, running water and some form of tables and chairs. With more than 10 vendors, you can choose from Latin food of Colombia, Honduras, El Salvador, Mexico, the Dominican Republic, Puerto Rico and Cuba. Try meats grilled a la plancha, tacos, homemade stews, sturdy mofongo (mashed and fried green plantain) or a Cuban sandwich of juicy roasted pork, ham, Swiss cheese, pickles and yellow mustard pressed crisp on French bread. There are juices and fresh fruit cups showered in chili spices, sugar-heavy Cuban coffee, snoballs and snacks. This is comfort food at its homey best, and there is much to try. Pace yourself; this journey is just beginning.

About a mile off the expressway, fresh pita bread is baking at Crescent Market. Well-stocked and neat-as-a-pin, the family-run market runs a pita-making operation in the back, turning out fresh, puffed loaves (the real deal!). There's also an on-site Halal butcher, stunning and unique produce and 15 food aisles with rice, dried fruits, dairy, candies and gorgeous sticky, syrup-soaked baklava. Leave with a bag of warm, za'atar-dusted flatbreads.

From there, head to Eclair Delicieux, neatly tucked in a tiny strip mall, food-spotting Latin and Vietnamese restaurants for future treks along the way. Chef Patty Dinh's cases are full of gorgeous

flan-topped cupcakes, waffle cookies, brûléed crêpe cakes or banana bread, nestled next to chocolates and loads of other innovative and interesting sweets.

Not far away, rising from the earth like a cement phoenix, is the expansive building that houses Hong Kong Market. A tour of this place is a global food adventure. Pass through the giant sliding-glass doors, grab a handbasket and head to the right toward the deli. Gawk at the barbecued duck and other cooked meats, wander among the packaged foodstuffs and steamed rice-flour buns and aisle after aisle of kitchen gadgets, cans, jars and bottled goods from across several continents, before hitting the wild snacks/sweets section, the vast produce department with intriguing fruits and vegetables, a forest of herbs and a mini café selling tiny Vietnamese banh xeo (stuffed crepes). Plan to be here a while, but save room . . . there's more.

Just alongside the Mississippi River, truly on its west bank, is Algiers Point, an old, venerated neighborhood that has long been dotted with great architecture, cafés, bars and coffee shops. Missing until now has been a market. Several months in, Faubourg Fresh Market broaches the grocery store game, albeit gently. The stash is predominantly locally sourced meats, breads, jams, spices, pickles and some prepared foods (get anything from the Thali Llama), mixed in with some usual grocery goods. A continuing work in progress, the number of stocked items grows daily, and the addition of locally made soaps and other crafts makes for neighborhood-market magic.

Go east for a trip across the river to New Orleans' Westbank, and explore the broad food heritage that makes up the city's cultural gumbo. Stir the pot, shop the markets, eat the food. Fork in hand, laissez les bons temps rouler.

COCHON BUTCHER

930 Tchoupitoulas Street
(504) 588-7675
cochonbutcher.com

Chef Donald Link was the first to open a new restaurant as part of the post-Katrina recovery. In April 2006, Cochon started serving the citified country food of Chef Donald and partner Chef Stephen Stryjewski. Set in a restored New Orleans warehouse, the restaurant feels like gussied-up rusticity—all wood furnishings and soothing warm food colors on the walls. The food is Louisiana comfort that can begin with wood-fired oyster roast or a bowl of smoked duck and tasso gumbo before shifting to a citrusy-beefy-earthy mushroom salad with deep-fried beef jerky and lemon vinaigrette, and meandering over to rabbit and dumplings or namesake Louisiana cochon with roasted turnip, cabbage, and cracklin'. It's for these dishes and their dedication to New Orleans that the chefs won a James Beard Award. Donald and Steven planned to open a shop for retailing the fresh meats they house-butchered, and other foodstuffs they made, so, not long after Cochon, came Cochon Butcher—a sandwich counter, butcher shop, and wine bar, rolled into one. People fell head over heels for the house-cured sausages and meats, pickles, mustard, and Cochon Muffuletta (to name one popular sandwich). The bacon pralines became legendary, as did the chocolate chip cookies that one local lawyer–food writer swears are a secret weapon designed by pastry chef Rhonda Ruckman to keep him hooked. The savory dishes at Butcher may be heavenly, but Rhonda's devilishly delectable pastry is a huge draw.

BREAD & BUTTER PICKLES

(YIELDS 7 QUARTS)

2 cups salt

1½ gallons water

1½ gallons ice

11 pounds cucumbers, in ⅛-inch slices

10 cups cider vinegar

10 cups sugar

½ cup mustard seed

2 tablespoons celery seed

2 tablespoons turmeric

2 tablespoons black pepper, coarsely ground

2 tablespoons red pepper flakes

2½ pounds onions, thinly sliced

Make brine with salt and water. Chill. Add ice. Pour ice-filled brine over cucumbers. Soak overnight in refrigerator. Combine vinegar, sugar, and spices. Bring to boil to melt sugar. Pack drained cucumbers and onions into sterilized jars, leaving ½ inch of space from top of jar. Pour pickling liquid to cover. Process 10 minutes.

COCHON'S PB&J COOKIES

(YIELDS 2-3 DOZEN)

For the Ponchatoula strawberry jam:

3 pints strawberries, washed, hulled, halved

1¼ cups granulated sugar, divided

Pinch of salt

½ tablespoon apple pectin

Lime juice to taste

For the peanut butter cookie dough:

2½ cups unbleached all-purpose flour

½ teaspoon baking soda

½ teaspoon baking powder

1 teaspoon table salt

½ pound (2 sticks) unsalted butter

1 cup packed dark brown sugar

1 cup granulated sugar

1 cup smooth peanut butter

2 large eggs

2 teaspoons vanilla extract

1 cup roasted salted peanuts, chopped

To make the jam: Place strawberries, 1 cup sugar, and salt in a sauce pot over low heat and simmer. Stir well and cook until the mixture has reduced.

Mix ¼ cup sugar and the pectin in a bowl. Sprinkle pectin mixture over simmering berries while stirring to prevent any lumps. Bring mixture back to a boil and remove from heat. Stir in lime juice.

Transfer to a container and place plastic wrap directly on surface of jam. When cool, refrigerate until set or overnight.

To prepare the dough: Preheat oven to 350°F. Sift flour, baking soda, baking powder, and salt into a medium bowl. Set aside.

In bowl of electric mixer with paddle attachment, cream together butter and sugars. Beat until fluffy, about 5 minutes, stopping to scrape down bowl as necessary. Mix in peanut butter until fully incorporated, then eggs, one at a time, and vanilla. Mix dry ingredients into peanut butter mixture with a spatula. Add ground peanuts. Mix until just incorporated.

To make the cookies: Working with 1 tablespoon of dough at a time, place in cup molds and flatten slightly. Add a tablespoon of jam to the center of each. Top with another tablespoon of dough. Bake until cookies are puffed and brown along edges, 14–16 minutes. Cool cookies until set, and remove from molds. Enjoy!

EMERIL'S

800 Tchoupitoulas Street
(504) 528-9393
emerilsrestaurants.com/emerils-new-orleans

Full disclosure, for ten years I was one of the writers for the Emerils.com blog. I adored working for Emeril and remember the days when he could be found sitting behind his paper-covered desk in the narrow home-base offices on Camp Street, eating a sandwich while plotting the future. Emeril

is a hero, an innovator, and damn killer cook, with an even more amazing palate. He opened his flagship restaurant in 1990 on a street that had gone fallow, in an area that was all but dead. That kind of dice-rolling smarts, combined with talent, is why he is a star. He also knows how to find great chefs to curry for his empire. Emeril's is an insanely busy restaurant where the food has gone from upticked southern favorites to all kinds of ethnic interpretations and back around

to original items again offered as part of Emeril's traditions. Always in step with what and how people eat, Emeril and his crew of chefs, cooks and staff help keep the menu fresh with local and regional produce, and of course locally sourced meats and seafoods. When they find a food item not from our region, bank on it that it's the best available. Pork fat may still rule, but Emeril knows how to lighten things up, so he offered this crudo (raw) recipe.

EMERIL'S SCALLOP CRUDO
Recipe Courtesy Emeril Lagasse
Emeril's Food of Love Productions, 2008
(SERVES 4 AS APPETIZER)

5 Maine day-boat scallops

2 limes

1 (8-ounce) Yukon Gold potato, peeled

1 (8-ounce) red beet, peeled

2 oranges

1 lemon

2 red grapefruits

⅛ teaspoon orange zest

2 tablespoons sugar

½ teaspoon Dijon mustard

¼ teaspoon prepared horseradish

3 tablespoons extra virgin olive oil

4 ounces thinly sliced guanciale

3 tablespoons American paddlefish caviar

2 tablespoons toasted pine nuts, for garnish

20 baby arugula leaves

12 thin slices radish

12 thin slices jalapeño

Slice each scallop crosswise into 4 thin slices. Squeeze the juice of 1 lime over the sliced scallops and allow them to marinate for 10–15 minutes in the refrigerator.

Using a Japanese spiral slicer, slice the potato and then the beet. Store each in a separate bowl of water in the refrigerator until ready to use.

Juice 1 orange, lemon, lime, and grapefruit; there should be about 1 cup of juice. Pour the juice into a medium saucepan and bring to a boil over high heat. Once the juice boils, reduce the heat to medium-low and stir in the zest and sugar. Steadily simmer the juice, stirring occasionally, until it has reduced to 3 tablespoons, about 25 minutes.

In a small mixing bowl, combine the juice reduction with the Dijon mustard and prepared horseradish. Slowly whisk in the olive oil until the mixture is emulsified. Set aside.

Remove the rind and the pith from the remaining grapefruit and orange. Using a paring knife, remove all of the segments and set aside.

Assemble the dishes on 4 cold plates. Remove the beets from the water and pat dry. Arrange ¼ cup of the beets on each plate. Evenly divide the scallops over the beets and then drizzle 1 tablespoon of the vinaigrette over each plate. Place 2 grapefruit segments and 2 orange segments around each plate. Divide the guanciale evenly into 4 servings and place around each plate. Remove the potatoes from the water and pat dry; place ¼ cup of potato over each plate. Place 2 teaspoons of caviar, in separate piles, over the potatoes, and sprinkle 1 teaspoon of pine nuts evenly over each dish. Arrange 5 baby arugula leaves on each dish and top with 3 slices each of radish and jalapeño.

BONUS RECIPE FROM CHEF LISA BARBATO

Because these tartlets are heavenly and this recipe is so worth the effort.
Follow Lisa on Instagram: @chasingforks

First I fell in love with buttery, flaky, herbaceous tomato tarts and then I fell in love with Lisa Barbato. Lisa is a cook's cook, an incredibly industrious and hardworking pastry chef, who doesn't mess around, though she refers to herself as "the anti-baker," relying more on feel, sight, scent, and taste than on a scale. She has worked the pastry station at some of the city's most important restaurants, including Anne Kearney's storied Peristyle and the Brennan family's Mr. B's Bistro, and in the post–August 2005 restaurant landscape she did a stint at the short-lived Alberta's. Her plated desserts have graced magazine covers, and her special-occasion cakes bring tears of joy. Lisa has serious passion for all things Italian and French, so at Christmas there is panettone and during Mardi Gras there are French (puff pastry and almond paste) and New Orleans-style traditional (brioche) King Cakes. Lisa became a regular fixture at Saturday's Crescent City Farmers Market in 2006, and since then has amassed a big fan base. Everything Lisa makes is from scratch, hand rolled, hand cut, filled and perfect. Fair warning: these tomato tarts are seriously addictive.

TOMATO TARTLETS ON HOMEMADE PUFF PASTRY

(YIELDS 12)

For puff pastry:

1 cup all-purpose flour

2 cups bread flour

2 teaspoons salt

1 tablespoon sugar

1 pound unsalted butter, at room temperature

1 cup cold water

For pesto (makes 1 cup):

4 cups fresh basil leaves

⅓ cups walnuts (optional)

2 cloves garlic

½ cup grated Parmesan cheese

1 teaspoon salt

½ cup olive oil (not extra virgin)

For tartlet topping:

¼ cup pesto

1 cup ricotta cheese

2 medium ripe tomatoes

1 cup grated Parmesan cheese

To make puff pastry: In the bowl of an electric mixer, place the flours, salt, sugar, and ¼ pound (1 stick) butter.

Add cold water and mix with the dough hook until a ball forms. Do not overmix. Turn out ball and wrap in cling film. Refrigerate for at least 6 hours or overnight.

Press the remaining ¾ pound of butter between two sheets of plastic wrap and form into a

¼-inch-thick square that's 4 x 4 inches. The butter must be softened but not too soft.

Once the dough has rested 6 hours or overnight, roll it out into a 6 x 6-inch square. Unwrap the butter block and lay it diagonally on the dough square. Fold in the edges, envelope style, then fold the resulting square in half to make a rectangle. Brush away any excess flour, wrap in plastic, and refrigerate for 25 minutes. Once rested in the refrigerator, roll out the dough into a 6 x 18-inch rectangle.

Fold each of the outer one-thirds over the center one-third to make a 6-inch square, then fold in half again to make a rectangle. Wrap and refrigerate for another 25 minutes.

Remove from the refrigerator and repeat the roll-and-fold one more time. Wrap well in plastic and refrigerate for at least 6 hours. This method creates all those delicious flaky layers.

Remove dough from refrigerator. Roll into a 16 x 12-inch rectangle. Using a 4-inch cookie cutter or pastry ring, cut 12 circles. Make a circle depression in each dough round using a slightly smaller (3-inch) ring. Be careful not to cut through the dough. This smaller ring will create an "edge" to hold the filling.

Place pastry rounds on a parchment-lined baking sheet and wrap well. Refrigerate for 1 hour or freeze to be used within one month.

To make pesto: Combine basil, nuts (if using), garlic, cheese, and salt in a blender or food processor. Pulse until mixed well. Add olive oil and pulse until paste forms.

To assemble and bake: Preheat oven to 425°F. Remove prepared dough from refrigerator. Top each dough round with a teaspoon each of pesto and ricotta. Top with a thin slice of tomato and sprinkle with 1–2 teaspoons of Parmesan cheese. Bake for 20 minutes, rotating once, until puff pastry is golden brown. Eat warm or let come to room temperature. Best eaten the day it's made.

INDEX

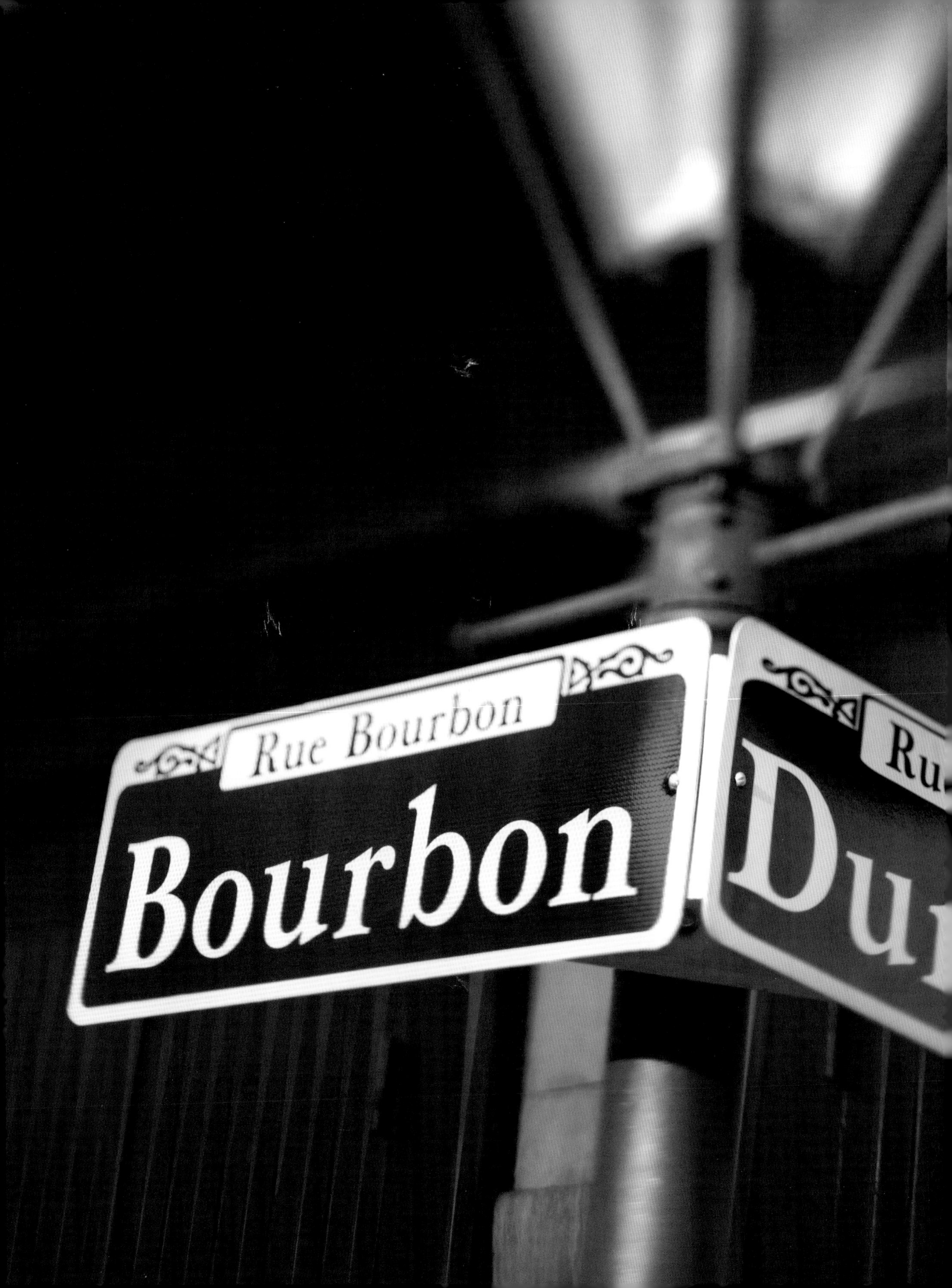
Rue Bourbon
Bourbon

ABOUT THE AUTHOR

Lorin Gaudin has passion for all things food, drink and arts. With a Bachelor's degree in Theatre from Loyola University of New Orleans, and a culinary diploma from The Ritz-Escoffier in Paris, she parlayed her education to become a Food Editor/Reporter for national, regional and local publications as well as local television and radio. Lorin is an adjunct instructor at Delgado Community College's Culinary program, teaching Menu Planning & Design, Food Writing, and Social Media. She also hosts a food radio show broadcasting from Delgado's radio station, WXDR 99.1FM. She is the Food Editor for *Where Magazine* New Orleans, and has written for Emeril, The *New York Post*, *New Orleans* Magazine, *Louisiana Cookin'*, GoNola.com and more. Lorin is the creator-founder of FiveOhFork, specializing in food journalism and culinary social media/web content for the culinary industry.

ABOUT THE PHOTOGRAPHER

Born in Mid-City New Orleans, **Romney Caruso** used the distinctiveness of his surroundings to train his eye in the art of alluring image creation. Through dedication to his craft, his skill garnered him numerous awards and brought him international attention. But true to the roots of the

environment he grew up in, he kept focus on the things that truly matter: love of family, great music, and superior food!

For years, Romney has brought to light the indelible imagery of New Orleans' cuisine. The richness of the pageantry and flair that accompanies this very unique gastronomy can only be matched with Romney's unforgettable photography that practically brings the taste of the food right off the page. This is accomplished through his genuine homegrown love of food, paired with his incomparable skill at capturing light and displaying the beauty of a true culinary masterpiece. His greatest joy is derived from working with the people he has met on his sessions including famous chefs, restaurateurs, and individuals from various walks of life.

—Ade Herbert